William F. Haynes Jr.

SEA TIME

William F. Haynes, Jr., M.D., Lieutenant, Medical Corps, USNR (1957)

SEA TIME

Life On Board Supply and Troop Ships
During World War II and Its Aftermath

by
William F. Haynes, Jr., M.D.

The Darwin Press, Inc.
Princeton, New Jersey

ISBN: 0-87850-167-3 (HARDBOUND)

Library of Congress Cataloging-in-Publication Data

Haynes, William F.
  Sea time : life on board supply and troop ships during World War II and its af-
termath / by William F. Haynes, Jr.
      p. cm.
  Includes index.
  ISBN 0-87850-167-3 (alk. paper)
  1. Haynes, William F. 2. World War, 1939-1945--Transportation. 3. World
War, 1939-1945--Naval operations, American. 4. World War, 1939-1945--
Personal narratives, American. 5. Merchant mariners--United States--
Biography. 6. Ship physicians--United States--Biography. I. Title.
  D810.T8H39 2006
  940.54'7573092--dc22
  [B]
                                                                    2006032797

Cover: SS *Bluefield Victory* at sea. Named after Bluefield College in Virginia, founded in 1922, the *Bluefield Victory* was constructed in the port of Los Angeles, California in 1944. (Photo: Courtesy of the U.S. Maritime Administration, Washington, D.C.)

Darwin® Books are printed on acid-free paper and meet the guidelines for permanence and durability of the Committee on production guidelines for Book Longevity of the Council on Library Resources.☉

Published by:
                    The Darwin Press, Inc.
              Box 2202, Princeton, NJ 08543-2202 USA
             Tel: (609) 737-1349 Fax: (609) 737-0929
                  E-mail: books@darwinpress.com
                   Web: www.darwinpress.com

                Printed in the United States of America

DEDICATED
TO THOSE SEAMEN
WHOSE SHIPS WERE RESPONSIBLE
FOR TRANSPORTING THE MUCH-NEEDED
TROOPS AND MATÉRIEL
TO TROUBLE SPOTS
AROUND THE GLOBE
DURING WORLD WAR II
AND ITS AFTERMATH

CONTENTS

ILLUSTRATIONS

Figures

Plates
(Plates follow page 46)

FOREWORD

The United States Merchant Marine and the United States Navy have a long history that goes back to the beginning of naval operations in the era of the American Revolution. In October 1775, the Continental Congress authorized two vessels, a galley and a frigate, to be armed and to search for British ships carrying munitions to the colonies. More ships were added during the Revolution; however, the Continental Congress, lacking funds, sold all the surviving vessels in 1785.

The Constitution of the United States of America (1789) then empowered the new Congress "to provide and maintain a navy," which Congress did in 1794 by commissioning six frigates that were high-speed scouting vessels, outfitting them with guns. In 1797, three newly built ships were launched, and Congress established the Department of the Navy in April 1798. These first ships were manned by ex-merchant mariners. From then on, the United States Navy and the American Merchant Marine evolved together. For the first 50 years, Naval officers and men were trained on merchant vessels, which provided an important Reserve and source of manpower thereafter for the Navy.

The United States Naval Academy at Annapolis was founded in 1845 and from then on became the primary training school for United States Naval officers. The Naval Reserve Act of 1925 authorized a Merchant Marine Naval Reserve (later MMNR) as a component part of the United States Navy.

The Merchant Marine Act of 1936 provided for the federal training of Merchant Marine officers. By March 15, 1938, the Merchant Marine Cadet Corps was founded under the auspices of the United States Maritime Commission with the training school located at Kings Point, Long Island, New York. The United States Merchant Marine Academy was dedicated on September 30, 1943, by President Franklin D. Roosevelt, who said, "The Academy serves the Merchant Marine as West Point serves the Army and Annapolis serves the Navy."

The mission of the Merchant Marine Academy is to train officers to serve the Merchant Marine, the Navy, and the Armed Forces in marine transportation during peace and war.

PREFACE

Archivists, historical societies, and citizens from all walks of life have an intense interest today in wartime memorabilia as a way of preserving our heritage as a nation. There continues to be a deep fascination in the World War II era and its aftermath despite the passage of 60 years since the end of the conflict.

Although many books and movies have recorded episodes of famous invasions and battles involving well-known warships during World War II, the purpose of this book is to allow you, the reader, to experience a microcosm of life at sea, the day-to-day events that constitute the existence and survival of those who sailed during this period. Noteworthy is the dedication of those individuals and ships involved in transporting much-needed troops and matériel to all the combat areas around the globe. This was the job of the Merchant Marine. It required a community of well-trained, ship-board personnel to complete the task. Aware of the enemy's hidden presence during any or all voyages and conscious of threats to the ship itself presented by an unpredictable ocean, they stood by the war effort with courage and determination, and indeed made victory at sea possible.

I have purposely avoided the major role of heroics, because in my case, fortunately, there was very limited action to report, except at Saipan. My task, however, is to bring to you the experience of life at sea. A portion of my narrative includes the war years while serving as a Cadet-Midshipman and junior deck officer aboard supply and troopships in the Pacific theater. Then later, as Third Mate on Troop Ships after Kings Point graduation in 1946 and again in the summer of 1947, I sailed as Third Mate on a cargo vessel bringing wheat to Europe under the Marshall Plan. During the years 1955 to 1957, I served on active duty as the Ship's Medical Officer aboard Navy transports crossing primarily the North Atlantic. The common denominator among many experiences in both theaters of operation centered around life at sea; hence, the title "Sea Time."

On a personal note, I want to mention that, during wartime, photographs and diaries were forbidden, and censorship of all letters was tight. Therefore, although I have attempted to remember details accurately, I did need to review my Naval and Merchant Marine records and various archives to determine the sequence of events. I plead in advance for forgiveness should the reader note some minor inaccuracies.

When a number of friends learned that I was writing about my voyages during and after the war, they became quite interested in the details. Some had spent time aboard naval vessels, some aboard cruise ships, and some raced sailboats on the ocean. One of my dear friends even admitted sheepishly to having fought ocean currents and waves in a row boat attempting to get back to the New Jersey shore. I hope they will enjoy reading these stories, even though many go back several decades.

Finally, I want to remember my grandchildren: Henri, Curtis, and Madeleine Hallé; Billy and Katie Haynes; and Eli, Lily, and Poppy Haynes. Attentive listeners all, as Pop-Pop related a number of sea stories at bedtime.

Acknowledgments

First and foremost, I am grateful for the vital encouragement and patience rendered to me by my good friend, Ed Breisacher, publisher of the Darwin Press. His ability to merge separate sections of the book into a cohesive story was, by any standards, a work of art and professional zeal. Our meetings were entertaining and covered many other items—from the state of the nation to the state of Princeton swimming. Thank you, Ed.

I am grateful to the Public Relations Department at the United States Merchant Marine Academy at Kings Point for the use of a few photos of activities taken from my graduation US-MMA Yearbook, *Midships, 1946.*

Captain Warren G. Leback, a 1944 graduate of the Academy and Maritime Administrator from 1989 to 1993, who is current Chairman of the Board of the Museum at Kings Point and loyal alumnus, gave his time to looking over the manuscript. I greatly appreciate his comments.

My classmate at the Academy and a long time friend, Lt. Commander Tom Reilly USNR (ret.), kindly refreshed my memory regarding convoys during World War II.

I am also indebted to Marty Skrocki, Public Information Officer, United States Merchant Marine Academy, for his time looking over the manuscript and suggesting corrections.

I want to acknowledge permission from Michael S. Yamashita, and Harmony House Publishers, Louisville, for two photographs from a fine book, *The United States Merchant Marine Academy*, published in 1988.

Lisa Donitz of the Alumni Affairs Office, United States Merchant Marine Academy, was always courteous and helpful.

My wife, Aline, has been able to look the other way, and sometimes close the door, when passing through my office cluttered with articles about ships, World War II photos, unfinished chapters, and other seafaring data scattered on the floor, tabletops, and bookcases. She has certainly earned a "plank" in the book's construction (a "plank" refers to a portion of a wooden deck, found on the old sailing ships) having been overall very understanding during this process. Thank you Aline!

NOTE: All color photographs in the plate section are from my personal collection of slides, except those cited in the legends under the photographs.

The black and white illustrations are from my personal collection of photographs with the exception of those cited in the legends.

I wish to acknowledge with thanks the assistance of Shannon M. Russell of the Maritime Administration, United States Department of Transportation, in Washington, D.C., and Lane Minerow, Esq. of the United States Department of Transportation, Maritime Administration, for permission to reproduce the photograph of the SS *Bluefield Victory* on the jacket. The *Bluefield Victory* was named after Bluefield College in Virginia, founded in 1922.

INTRODUCTION

This book resulted from my discovery a few years ago of a dusty old steamer trunk in the basement of my home. The trunk belonged to my mother, now deceased, and was jam-packed with letters I had sent her while I was serving as a Kings Point Cadet-Midshipman in the United States Merchant Marine. Still a teenager, I served on board the supply ship SS *Cape Catoche* in the Pacific theater during 1944 and 1945.

There were additional letters, separately wrapped and held together by an elastic band, dealing with my subsequent service as a Deck Officer on the troopship SS *Maritime Victory* between March and September 1946, where our mission was to return former German and Italian POWs to Europe, 1,500 at a time, and bring home a similar number of United States troops. As the Third Officer, I stood the 12 a.m. to 4 a.m. (2400 to 0400) watch, and the noon to 4 p.m. (1200 to 1600) watch. (The standard sea watches consist of four hours on duty and eight hours off duty.) The photos, papers, and other memorabilia in the trunk all related to the daily lives and cares of the crew and people we were transporting.

Fortunately, I also spotted my diary in the bottom of the same trunk. It was filled with more stories and additional photographs I had saved while serving during a summer trip in 1947 as Third Mate on the SS *Warwick Victory*, delivering wheat to Europe as part of this nation's Marshall Plan. I had just finished my freshman year at Princeton and remained in the Navy Reserve during my undergraduate years at the university, rising to the rank of Lt. (jg.) officer. I also completed a few Navy correspondence courses in my spare time and did a brief stint teaching navigation to enlisted men on board a destroyer escort tied up alongside a pier in Jersey City, an activity I discontinued when the pre-med demands became more important.

Upon graduation from Princeton in 1950, I moved on to medical school at the College of Physicians & Surgeons (P&S), Columbia University in New York City. My Kings Point classmates not already on active duty with the Navy were undoubtedly called up for duty during the Korean War, but the Navy preferred that I finish medical school and one year's medical internship before being called back for duty. My new role would be that of Navy physician rather than Deck Officer. This came true following graduation from P&S in 1954 and completion of a medical internship at St. Luke's Medical Center in New York by July 1, 1955. The Navy's orders arrived promptly.

Despite my hope that I would be assigned to a battleship or aircraft carrier, I was ordered to report to . . . (you guessed it!) . . . a troop ship, the USNS *General Harry Taylor* as Ship's Medical Officer. Thus began a succession of five different troopship assignments over a period of two years, under the aegis of the Military Sea Transport Service (MSTS) headquartered in Brooklyn, New York.

The *Taylor* carried 1,500 troops to Bremerhaven and about the same number on the return trip to New York. The ship had a remarkable record during World War II carrying troops and supplies to almost every area of conflict. After I had completed several voyages on the *Taylor,* I was transferred to a second vessel when the *Taylor* was sent in for major maintenance.

The Navy Commandant at the Brooklyn Navy Yard, who was responsible for assigning physicians to various ships at this time, then notified me that I was to report for three weeks of Temporary Assigned Duty (TAD) on the USS *General George M. Randall*, an all-Navy ship, yet still part of the MSTS fleet. She resembled a modern passenger ship: She was fast, had two stacks, and was up-to-date. The mission was the same: transporting troops and dependents from New York to Europe and back.

At the conclusion of my three-week stint on the *Randall*, my next ship assignment was the USNS *General W.C. Langfitt*. The mission of the *Langfitt* was most unique: She was to collect and transport 2,500 men, women, and children on each voyage to this country. All of these passengers were escapees from the many "Iron Curtain" countries during the year 1955 to 1956, and they were sponsored by various secular and church groups in the United States. The Commandant of MSTS required a minimum of three round-trip voyages on the *Langfitt* before the ship's Medical Officer could apply for transfer to another vessel. These trips were most interesting, and at times heart-breaking. After making 12 round-trip voyages with very short turn-around times and having done more than the minimum three voyages as required, I was quite exhausted and requested to be transferred off the *Langfitt* . The Commandant offered me the opportunity to go ashore at a Navy recruiting center, but this did not beckon. I preferred being at sea.

My request to stay at sea was rewarded with two voyages on the USNS *Pvt. Elden H. Johnson.* This was a smaller vessel and therefore carried fewer troops and dependents; in addition, the vessel plied the beautiful waters of the Caribbean, with stops at Guantanamo Bay (Cuba), San Juan (Puerto Rico), and Panama City (Panama). The weather was balmy and pleasant, and the waters calm—a welcome change from the often rough and tumble North Atlantic.

My final tour, awarded by the Commandant at MSTS, lasted nine months (from 1956 to 1957) on one of the newest troop ships in the United States Navy, the USNS *Geiger.* As Ship's Medical Officer, my duties now involved responsibility for the well-being of 1,500 United States troops and dependents being transported from New York to Bremerhaven, Germany, where they were to take up new stations in Europe. Then, we would return 1,500 troops and dependents to the United States. Also, one of the trips took me to Southampton (England) and back on the same type of mission.

The Ship as a Community
Like the members of a small-town community, the personnel who comprise the ship's crew derive from diverse backgrounds. It is therefore imperative that all crew members cooperate in a harmonious way, following orders, addressing concerns, and making the best of every situation while utilizing their individual skills.

Passengers will often experience a number of side effects from just being at sea. Seasickness, in the opinion of those so afflicted, is the nearest thing to dying. Among those who belong to the ship's company, seasickness is fortunately rare. Aside from passenger *mal de mer*, there were other unexpected challenges, such as the sudden appearance of wandering icebergs in the shipping lanes (often seen in April in the North Atlantic). Other concerns could include nearby vessels in the shipping lanes, rocky or shallow coastlines, and an unpredictable ocean with its huge waves and storms.

Wartime conditions bring their own set of concerns such as enemy attacks by air, surface ships, and submarines as well as the danger of floating mines. Unfortunately, one would hear about an occasional Liberty ship breaking apart during times of rough weather, but evidently this was rare. Another wartime concern for many ships was the lack of radar navigation equipment. This became a major concern for me when I was the Watch Officer navigating the English Channel in a pea-soup fog on a ship carrying 1,500 troops, an experience never to be forgotten. (I will mention this in more detail later).

Each part or section of this book represents an individual microcosm about individuals who, knowingly or not, contributed to history in the making. There are three parts to *Sea Time*:

Part I explains the background of the war and provides images from early memories of the wartime home front as well as Kings Point and the Academy.

Part II is concerned with the role of supply and troopships during World War II in the South Pacific, and my service as a Cadet-Midshipman, followed by trips to Europe immediately after the war as a Deck Officer (Third Mate).

Part III consists of experiences encountered as Ship's Medical Officer on Navy Ships belonging to the MSTS between 1955 and 1957. Being the sole physician, I was responsible for the health and well-being of all on-board. Most of these trips on various ships included transporting 1,500 troops, often with dependents. But one ship stands out as unique and special, having an important role in the history of this period. This ship was the USNS *General W.C.*

Langfitt whose mission, as previously mentioned, was to transport refugees from Iron Curtain countries as well as other refugees who had escaped during the Hungarian revolution.

Although I discuss journeys on several different ships, each voyage was influenced by the nature of the mission at hand, the state of world affairs, and many unpredictable events associated with traveling the high seas. By the end of the book, those of you who have experienced some sea time, may have similar memories of the perils of the sea and wonders of the deep. For those with little or no time aboard ocean-going ships, I hope you may gain a clearer idea of some of the daily challenges to be found there.

Ocean travel may invoke both a love-hate relationship, but one thing is certain: no two days are the same.

PART I

Background and Service with the United States Merchant Marine

Fig. 1. The USS *Arizona* was one of the primary targets of the Japanese attack on Pearl Harbor, December 7, 1941. (Source: National Archives, Washington, D.C.)

Chapter 1:

America at War: Personal Reflections and Images from the Home Front

How well I remember the disturbing world news on that cold, raw, mid-December morning in 1943, as I stood on the street corner waiting for the trolley to take me to school. The radio had just finished broadcasting sobering details of the war. I was seventeen and a senior at Newark Academy, a boy's day school. There were many school activities planned for that day; yet, there seemed to be a curtain of uncertainty, ever present, even during the busy school-day activities. There was little doubt that most of my classmates and I would be in uniform by the time our class graduated in June of 1944.

The trolley ride from my home in Orange, New Jersey, to Newark usually lasted 30 minutes, more than enough time to stew about things military. Several questions kept sailing through my head: What branch of the service would I choose and why and where and when?

Two years had already passed since Japan's surprise attack on Pearl Harbor on December 7, 1941. The highly successful surprise strike against our Pacific fleet was a disaster for the United States.[1] Eighteen of our warships were sunk or badly damaged (Fig. 1);

---

[1] Only 40 years later did some of us realize that the objective of crippling the United States fleet in the Pacific was to prevent the United States from interfering militarily in Japan's grand strategy of expanding its empire by possessing all the British, Dutch, French, and Portuguese territories in the Far East, along with all their combined natural resources. The subsequent annexation of the Philippines, India, and Australia was also being considered. At some point in time following the occupation of the above territories, Japan's goal was then to negotiate for a peace with the United States, while still retaining control of its Far East Empire.

3

2,400 sailors were killed, 1,300 were wounded, and 230 planes were destroyed on the ground.

The day following the attack, President Franklin D. Roosevelt, with the backing of Congress, declared war against Japan. He proclaimed in words that I shall never forget: "Yesterday, December 7, 1941—a date which will live in infamy—the United States of America was suddenly and deliberately attacked by naval and air forces of the Empire of Japan." Since both Germany and Italy had signed a Tripartite Treaty with Japan the previous year, it came as no surprise that on December 11, 1941, both Italy and Germany likewise declared war against the United States. These events marked the beginning of World War II, a conflict that involved many countries around the globe in a brutal war that would last almost four more years.

War-Time Images on the Home Front

Many wartime images from the early 1940s remain in my memory while growing up in New Jersey. These include: gas rationing; saving aluminum foil; repairing holes in socks; collecting three-cent stamps, many of which illustrated various wartime events; and buying Government War Bonds. (I received a war Bond from my Aunt on my 16th birthday; it cost $18 and would be worth $25 in ten years.) Searchlights actively scanned the night skies for enemy bombers that might be flying over our Orange, New Jersey, neighborhood. Lights from New York skyscrapers were darkened because they were found to silhouette our convoys at night as they crept along the Atlantic coast—easy targets for lurking Nazi U-boats. Civilian Defense volunteers patrolled the streets and directed people to the nearest air-raid shelters during drills. Our cellars now held canned foods and water. During practice air raids, students were taught to crouch under their desks.

Newscasters such as Gabriel Heater, Raymond Gram Swing, and Edward R. Murrow carried radio reports of the conflict from around the world. Newsreels inside the movie houses brought

Pl. 2

Pl. 3

Fig. 2. Uncle Sam Wants You. (Source: Original poster painted circa 1916 by James Montgomery Flagg. Adapted for use in World War II.)

Fig. 3. Rosie the Riveter: Women power during World War II. (Source: Commissioned by the United States War Production Coordinating Committee as a recruiting poster in 1943. Artist J. Howard Miller.)

home the action in black-and-white film strips of battles being fought by our troops.

My mother wore a colorful Royal Canadian Air Force cap as she drove off to work. She was the Elementary Supervisor of the five Orange public schools, and her mandate was teaching reading readiness.

My aunt enlisted in the Waves and was a Navy petty officer working as a meteorologist at the Lakehurst Naval Air Station in New Jersey.

One recruiting poster depicted "Uncle Sam" pointing his finger at the reader and stating: "Uncle Sam Wants You!" (Fig. 2). Another popular poster displayed "Rosie the Riveter" (Fig. 3), dedicated to the many women working in the defense industries. Another poster revealed a young soldier and his date dining in a restaurant; under the table was a cartoon of Hitler listening for possible United States military plans: "Loose talk can sink a ship" was the warning on the sign.

A common sight while traveling down "Main Street USA" was a small banner displaying one or more stars in windows of many homes: A blue star meant that a family member was in the service; a gold star announced that a family member had been killed serving his or her country.

"Victory gardens" were encouraged on any vacant piece of land to enable owners to raise their own produce. The entire nation was united in the war effort.

The Nineteen Forties: Great Songs and Great Bands

With America fully engaged in World War II, the nineteen forties was a time of great melodies: some tender, some uplifting, some bringing an air of hope.

Can any of us ever forget the songs and singers, and bands of this era? Glen Miller's "In the Mood," never seems to have lost its appeal. But once I was in uniform, the songs took on a more personal meaning such as "I Don't Want to Walk Without You," by Harry James, or "Sentimental Journey" by Les Brown with Doris Day. "It's been a Long, Long, Time," was another hit recording by

Harry James creating a yearning for family and one's current girl friend.

For us, these songs conveniently lent themselves to "touch dancing," a name given by a number of the young members of the current generation. It might be argued that the fox trot and slow moving close dancing of our days has given way to an aerobic workout on the dance floor with both partners distanced from each other: The importance of rhythm seems to have superseded melody. Perhaps I sense a transformation to the old style of our days, by the above young set, or is this wishful thinking?

Yet today, I can usually associate a certain song with a certain time and place. This is especially true when I hear a recording of Jimmy Dorsey's rendition: "There'll be Bluebirds over the White Cliffs of Dover." I never dreamed that at some time in the distant future, I would relive this song personally. It all began in 1955, while serving in the Navy as Ship's Medical Officer on troopships. I could almost set my watch as we sighted the White Cliffs. Almost like clockwork, the ship's loudspeaker would bark: "Dr. Haynes, report to the main deck immediately." Upon arrival at the scene, I found a soldier, one of 1,500 troops we were bringing back to the States, confused, barely responsive, lying on the deck, and showing signs of acute alcohol withdrawal. Explanations for these mysterious happenings will be described later.

Lastly, volumes of wonderful songs have been recorded that helped this country keep going during World War II. One such classic remains in my memory, and that was Kate Smith's singing "God Bless America" on the occasion of a patriotic gathering. She was a big woman with a big heart, and had the ability to really belt out the words.

Now for the Story

Now that the general background of the war has been sketched in, there is one more most important and indispensable element to the story: the United States Merchant Marine Academy (Kings Point). Kings Point was for me the beginning of a series of experiences and challenges oriented around the sea.

Fig. 4. Kings Point cadets standing in formation: Saturday morning Regimental Review. (Source: *A Pictorial Review of Kings Point,* United States Merchant Marine Academy, n.d.)

Chapter 2:

The United States Merchant Marine Academy at Kings Point

In December 1943, I applied for appointment to the United States Merchant Marine Academy at Kings Point as a chosen path to becoming an officer. I had always enjoyed being on the ocean while visiting friends at the New Jersey shore during summer vacations, and through the years I always had a positive feeling about the Navy. Even as a child one of my favorite radio programs was "Don Winslow of the United States Navy."

As is the case for all service academies, there were then, and still are, certain academic and physical qualifications to be fulfilled before acceptance, including a Congressional appointment. When applying to Kings Point, newcomers were given the choice of entering as either deck cadets or engine cadets. Having neither the interest nor the talent regarding engines, I chose "deck cadet." It also had occurred to me that I would be better off not being in the engine room should we be torpedoed. Little did I realize that the casualty rate for those working on deck was about the same as that for those in the engine room.

The required paperwork was filled in; the Congressional appointment was obtained; and the whole package was mailed to Kings Point around the early part of January 1944. A few weeks later, I was shocked to receive a letter stating that I was to report in February 1944 for a Navy physical at 90 Church Street in New York City, Headquarters of the Third Naval District. I showed up and passed the physical. There were academic requirements that I fulfilled, and my acceptance to Kings Point was soon in the mail.

A few weeks later, another surprise! I was to report in mid-

9

March 1944, to begin officer training as a plebe! My great plans to be able to finish my senior year had apparently evaporated. I was, however, allowed by Newark Academy's administration to take special "final exams" allowing me to graduate "in absentia" with the rest of the class in June 1944. Fortunately, I passed the exams.

As I stood alone in Newark's Penn Station with bags in hand, the stark reality of a "global war" suddenly had become "personal." My life was changing—much sooner than I had expected. The train took me from Newark to Manhattan, where I boarded another train for Great Neck, Long Island, a village adjacent to Kings Point. The last link involved a bus ride along "Steamboat Drive" that terminated at the impressive entry gates of the United States Merchant Marine Academy, well guarded by men in splendid uniforms. I had arrived at Kings Point, still 17 years of age, only a few weeks after my acceptance. It seemed that my life was moving at an increasingly fast pace. As I passed through the gates, I discovered that my name was already on a list of new plebes. The process of reporting for duty had begun. New sections of plebes periodically arrived, composed of engine cadets or deck cadets. I was one of 25 deck cadets in our section, known as Section PO-23.

Pl. 1

The Kings Point Program
The United States Merchant Marine Academy (USMMA) was established in January 1941 at Kings Point, New York, by the shores of Long Island Sound, on the grounds of the former Chrysler estate. In 1942, the training program was transferred to the War Shipping Administration (WSA) under the command of Admiral Emory Scott Land. The United States Merchant Marine Academy was dedicated in September 1943, and thus Kings Point became the fourth federal service academy, the other three being: West Point, which served the Army; the Naval Academy, which served the Navy; and the Coast Guard Academy.[2]

---

[2] In the United States today there are five federal service academies: West Point (1802), the Naval Academy (1845), the Coast Guard Academy (1932), the United States Merchant Marine Academy at Kings Point (1943), and the Air Force Academy (1954). In addition, there are six state Maritime Academies under federal supervision. These are: California Maritime Academy (Vallejo, CA); Great Lakes Maritime Academy (Traverse City, MI); Maine Maritime

Today Kings Point has a well established four-year program that consists of one year at sea and three years at the Academy. Upon graduation one is eligible for a B.S. degree, and a commission as an ensign in the reserve component of the United States Armed Forces. (By submitting additional liberal arts credits accumulated as a student at Princeton, I applied for, and received, a retroactive B.S. in Marine Transportation from Kings Point.) Likewise, exams were given by the United States Coast Guard in order to earn a license as a Third Mate in my case, or Third Assistant Engineer for those who were "engine" cadets.

Kings Point Cadets in Wartime

Kings Point is the only federal academy that has earned the right to carry a "battle standard," which is a small flag carried between the Stars and Stripes and the Academy flag while on parade. This is because Kings Point students served during World War II as junior officers aboard American flag ships in all areas of conflict, a mode of training that continues to this day. Other federal academies do not send undergraduates into combat before graduation.

There are a number of stories about the Kings Point cadets assigned to ships during World War II. To give a few examples: One cadet became a POW of the Japanese and survived the infamous Bataan Death March. A cadet from another graduating class had his ship torpedoed bringing supplies to Murmansk and was rescued from the icy waters, but unbelievably, while he was returning home aboard yet another vessel, this additional ship was also torpedoed, and once more he was rescued. Another cadet's ship was torpedoed in the Pacific theater; he subsequently spent 19 days in a life boat before being rescued. It is also significant to point out that 142 Kings Point cadets lost their lives in combat.

A close friend and member of my section at the Academy had his ship struck amidships by a kamikaze plane during the Philip-

Academy (Castine, ME); Massachusetts Maritime Academy (Buzzards Bay, MA); Seattle Maritime Academy (Seattle, WA); and SUNY Maritime College (Throgs Neck, NY). All of the academies currently enjoy a four-year program, prepare officers for their respective services, and are co-ed; however, only Kings Point Cadet-Midshipmen are placed on ocean-going vessels traveling around the globe while still undergraduates.

pine invasion, causing a fire and significant structural damage. The fire was brought under control, and the ship remained afloat and was able to limp back to Pearl Harbor.

There are presently two paintings hanging in the museum at Kings Point, both honoring the memory of Cadet-Midshipman Edwin J. O'Hara. O'Hara's Liberty ship, the *Stephen Hopkins*, was Pl. 4 attacked in the south Atlantic by the German auxiliary cruiser *Stier* and her escort, the *Tannenfels*, on September 17, 1942. In the ensuing battle, while his ship was sinking and the naval crew had all been killed, O'Hara continued to load and fire his remaining 4-inch shells and single-handedly scored hits on both German ships. The *Stier* sank under the waves but the damaged *Tannenfels* made port in Bordeaux. The *Stephen Hopkins* also went down. O'Hara died of shrapnel wounds, but fifteen members of the crew survived and were able to make it into a lifeboat, sailing more than 1,000 miles before reaching the safety of a small fishing port in Brazil.[3]

Morton Dietz, originally from Trenton, New Jersey, was the subject of an article,[4] which in part mentioned that, as a Cadet-Midshipman in World War II, his ship was torpedoed and sunk; he subsequently spent 31 days adrift in a lifeboat in the South Indian Ocean before being rescued at sea.

In a Commencement Address to the Class of 1992 at Kings Point, on June 15, 1992, General Colin Powell, Chairman of the Joint Chiefs of Staff, said, "Let there be no doubt among any in this audience: America is eternally grateful to all those who served in our merchant marine over the years—grateful for their efforts, their commitments, and their sacrifice in defense of our beloved America. They are second to none."

Such is some of the history of the Merchant Marine Cadet Corps—to cite only a few acts of heroism in the line of duty that became a part of Academy lore.

---

[3] The Merchant Marine Distinguished Service Medal, the highest medal for service beyond the call of duty, was awarded to 140 mariners (i.e., anyone sailing on a United States Merchant Marine ship in World War II). Seven were cadets from the United States Merchant Marine Academy (Kings Point), including Edwin O'Hara.

[4] "For World War II Vet (finally), Fight Never Ended," by Douglas Kalajian, Wednesday, April 5, 2000. Courtesy *Palm Beach Post* (Florida).

Casualties of War

Although the exact count of U.S. flag merchant ships lost in combat in World War II cannot be accurately determined, the closest figures suggest that 1,554 such ships were sunk due to war conditions, including 733 ships of over 1,000 gross tons. Things were especially bad in 1942, when, on average, 32 Allied ships in the Atlantic were sunk each week. During 1941 and 1942, the German Navy sank 2,963 Allied vessels, their objective being to sink as many ships as possible to prevent supplies and equipment from reaching England.[5]

More than 9,500 merchant mariner seamen were killed and 12,000 wounded, of whom 1,100 died from their wounds. There were 663 mariners who became POWs, with 66 dying in Japanese prison camps. It has been reported that one in 26 merchant marine sailors died in the line of duty, a greater percentage of wartime deaths than those suffered by any of the other U.S. military services.

It was only in 1988, 43 years after World War II, that the United States government officially granted veteran status to those mariners who served during the war.

Admiral Ugaki's Sword

Hundreds of Academy graduates were deck and engine officers aboard American merchant ships in the gigantic fleet that backed up every operation in the Pacific, including the final surrender and occupation of the Japanese home islands. In solemn recognition of

Fig. 5. Admiral Ugaki's sword.
(Source: http://www.usmm.org/ccsword.html.)

their service, the sword of Vice Admiral Ugaki, who commanded the Japanese Naval Forces of Northern Honshu and Hokkaido, was forwarded to the Merchant Marine Academy by General Douglas

---

[5] U.S. Merchant Marine web site: www.usmm.net/battleatlantic.html.

MacArthur. MacArthur wrote, "I have directed that the surrendered sword of Vice Admiral Ugaki, who commanded Japanese
Naval forces of Northern Honshu and Hokkaido, be forwarded to
the U.S. Merchant Marine Cadet Corps Academy, Kings Point,
New York, as a memento of the valiant services rendered by the
sons of this Academy in our struggle in the Pacific."[6]

The Cadet-Midshipman Goes to Sea

The war was at its peak, and a sense of strict discipline pervaded
our tight training organization and enveloped the entire Academy
during that March of 1944. An intensive "accelerated training program" was in full swing. Instead of four years, this was shortened
to two years due to an urgent need for more Merchant Marine officers because early on more ships were being sunk than able to be
replaced by the over-worked shipyards.

There were 3,891 cadets in 1944 when I arrived, including
those at sea. Because all the barracks were occupied, our section,
along with a few other sections, was assigned to an old sailing ship,
the TV *Emory Rice*, tied up permanently at one of the Academy's
piers (Fig. 6). Accommodations on the *Rice* included double-decker
metal beds and a slew of hammocks suspended by ropes from the
overhead beams. Most every night I could hear a dull "thump" followed by a groan, as someone in a hammock rolled over and landed
on the wooden deck.

Living on the *Rice* while tied up at the pier, we endured a
number of inconveniences such as stoking the ship's furnace with
coal, swabbing the decks, cleaning the head, arising very early, and

---

[6] The picture and the text about Admiral Ugaki's sword are excerpted from
www.usmm.org/ccsword.html and are copyrighted by that organization:
     www.usmm.org ©1998, 1999, 2000 U.S. Maritime Service Veterans.
   Vice Admiral Matome Ugaki became the leading Japanese Naval Commander
after Admiral Yamamoto was killed when his bomber was shot down by American fighters on April 18, 1943 near Bougainville in the Solomon Islands.
(Admiral Yamamoto was in command of the fleet that perpetrated the attack on
the United States military installation at Pearl Harbor, Honolulu, Hawaii, on
December 7, 1941.) Vice Admiral Ugaki was in a second bomber on the same
flight and was also shot down but survived. Admiral Ugaki was lost at sea when
the plane he was piloting was shot down attempting a kamikaze attack off the
coast of Okinawa on August 15, 1945—after Japan had unofficially surrendered.

Fig. 6. TV *Emory Rice*, underway before being permanently moored for a number of years at a pier at Kings Point. (Source: *A Pictorial Review of Kings Point,* United States Merchant Marine Academy, n.d.)

still attending classes. Taps was sounded at 10 p.m., and I was perpetually tired. While marching from one class to another, I would look at the green lawns and yearn to lie down for a nap.

As Cadet-Midshipmen, we carried a heavy load of courses such as seamanship, naval science, signaling, navigation, physical education, lifeboat handling, marching drills, meteorology, ship construction, shipping economics, and gunnery: all together, somewhere around 17 courses. The three-month plebe time was a vigorous period, mentally and physically, and we were relieved when we finally reached the end of our training in June 1944.

The Academy training policy has always involved "hands-on-learning at sea," combined with learning in the classroom. Since we were part of "wartime classes," an accelerated program, we spent three months as plebes before setting out on board an armed merchant ship for a minimum of six months transporting troops, military matériel, or supplies. My sea-time academic assignment included a "Sea Project" similar to a thesis; it contained an enormous number of questions, including required drawings. This was to be completed onboard the SS *Cape Catoche*, and the finished work was to be handed in at the conclusion of a minimum of six months at sea: my "Sea Time."

PART II

From Cadet-Midshipman to Deck Officer
(1944 to 1947)

Fig. 7. The SS *Cape Catoche*, a C-1 type vessel similar to the above, was built by the Consolidated Steel Corporation in Wilmington, California, in March 1944. She was 417 feet long by 60 feet wide with a draft of 38 feet. She could travel at 14 knots on 4,000 hp, and the gross tonnage was 6,750. There were five holds and covering hatches. The three decks were welded steel and the outside frame was riveted. The power was generated by a two-cycle steam turbine; her fuel oil capacity was 1,241 tons. (Official U.S. Coast Guard photograph. Courtesy: The Mariner's Museum, Newport News, Virginia.)

Chapter 3:

SS *Cape Catoche* (1944–1945)

First Voyage (1944)

In June 1944, about the time my class at Newark Academy was graduating, I was one of a dozen cadets bouncing along on a troop train heading for the West Coast. For a fleeting moment I wondered how my Newark classmates were doing. But this thought quickly switched from Newark Academy to the more immediate issues about the type of ship each of us would be assigned and what its destination would be. There was a sense of youthful excitement and some eagerness knowing that it would be a new adventure, and we would be heading to various ports in one or more of the war zones somewhere in the Pacific theater. The ships would most likely be oil tankers or vessels transporting war supplies. Upon arriving in San Francisco, we all parted company, wished each other good luck, and reported to our respective ships.

I felt a bit uneasy and quite alone, a stranger in a strange place. I had never been to the West Coast, nor had I spent any time on an ocean-going ship. The taxi let me off at the foot of the pier where the SS *Cape Catoche* was docked. After trudging along the lengthy pier, and hanging on to a large sea bag, I spotted the name *Cape Catoche* etched in the stern. She turned out to be a supply ship tied up at the very end of the wharf. Approaching her, I noticed stevedores working the booms and loading supplies and equipment into all of the ship's five holds. The smell of the stagnant water mixed with the musty odor found inside the warehouse combined to give a strange sense of the unfamiliar. As I drew nearer, I spotted whiffs of white smoke drifting lazily upward from the ship's smokestack. The *Catoche* was being readied to go, and it reminded me of an athlete at the ready, waiting for the starting gun. The gangway was quite steep, signaling that the ship was not yet filled with all her cargo. This was confirmed by noting that the free board, i.e., the distance from the deck to the waterline, was still high. Arriving at the foot of the gangway, I was impressed by her appearance; she was quite beautiful—yes, even "distinguished." Like all ships, the hull and the superstructure had been painted battleship gray, which served as camouflage when at sea.

Thick rope hawsers led from the *Catoche* and secured her to the pier. Rat guards were fastened in place, wrapped around the hawsers. I caught a glimpse of a cannon in place on the fantail—a suggestion of more weaponry that I would soon learn about. She had a set of booms located in the rear of the middle section of the ship that were busily loading matériel into the rear two holds. There were a pair of kingposts as well as another set of booms responsible for filling the forward three holds. As I recall, the midships of the *Catoche* contained crew's quarters as well as passageways both on the port side and on the starboard side connecting the bow area and stern area.

The deck above the crew's quarters housed the officers. The wheelhouse and the Captain's quarters were located at the next highest level. Finally, the "flying bridge" was atop that level, open to the elements, an area I found to be a meditative, quiet place when off duty, especially when the ocean was cooperative. The ship's stack, located behind the midships structure, was prominent here, as well as the ship's whistle.

I struggled up the steep gangway hanging on to my heavy luggage and trying to hide my shortness of breath as I neared the top. Reaching the ship's main deck, I was heartened to note that the *Catoche* was really tidy, with no trash to be seen anywhere.

It now became apparent to me that, having followed orders as a plebe (when a member of a group of cadets), things were to be different on the *Catoche*. Orders coming from one of the ship's officers would now be addressed to me personally. This would be a new experience, a step up in responsibility, a challenge accepted at this time with some uncertainty.

The vessel was only six months old and was a C-1 type of ship. For each class of vessels, the individual ships are frequently given a set of similar names. There were dozens of such C-1 ships, and most were named for a specific geographic Cape found in North America. The SS *Cape Catoche* was named for a small piece of land located at the extremity of the Yucatan Peninsula in southeast Mexico. A sampling of names of other "Cape" ships included SS *Cape Canaveral,* SS *Cape Cod*, SS *Cape Fear*, SS *Cape Greig*, SS *Cape Romano*, and so forth.[7]

It was somewhat comforting to learn that Cape ships, with their flexible riveted construction, were not plagued by technical problems with the hull, as were the rapidly constructed Liberty ships, and therefore were eminently seaworthy even after long exposure to rough, cold seas. The Cape ships were welded as well as riveted, which allowed them more flexibility in heavy seas, reducing the possibility of a serious failure.

My orders stated that I was to report immediately to the ship's Captain. One of the *Catoche*'s 25 Navy Armed Guard sailors directed me to his cabin. I knocked on his cabin door, and a voice within replied, "Come in." I entered and introduced myself. Captain Sanders was a sturdy man who, I later learned, was born in Estonia. He appeared to be about 60 years old and was around 5 feet 10 inches tall, with a good crop of graying hair. His gruff voice seemed to match his coarse veneer, and I detected a definite accent. After signing my orders and speaking a few words of welcome aboard, he then pointed me in the direction of the First Officer, alternately called the "Chief Mate," a wiry man in his early fifties with signs of a broken nose that made for a rough appearance. It crossed my mind: "Could this be a residue from a bar room brawl?" He was less than congenial, and very involved getting the deck gang ready for the voyage. But after a very brief introduction, he referred me to the Bos'n (Boatswain). This gentleman was also in his early fifties and, like the Captain, was about 5 feet 10 inches tall. He also displayed an ample supply of graying hair; he was trim, very quick on his feet, and was busy giving orders to the deck

---

[7] I have since read that Cape Catoche was the first Mexican land seen by the Spanish in 1517. Friar Diego de Landa noted in 1566, "Yucatan is the country with the least earth that I have ever seen, since it is all living rock" ("Yucatan's Ancient Roots," *Columbia Encyclopedia*, 6th ed. 2004). I had no knowledge of the history of the land when reporting on board, but I would not forget the admonition: "Navigational errors can land your ship on the rocks!"

sailors under his direction. A key ring with dozens of keys fastened to his belt sent a message that he was an important member of the crew. He had been a seaman all of his adult life and mirrored the common red face seen among ranchers and others working in the outdoor vocations or professions—or those who just had enjoyed a few "shots" of whiskey on a regular basis. The ship's maintenance and the efficiency of all the deck equipment were his major responsibilities.

Preparing to Put Out to Sea

The very next day the Bos'n introduced me to the fine art of chipping and scraping rusty areas at various locations on deck. The sequence still remains quite clear to me, after 60 years: 1) Chip and scrape away the rust, 2) apply lead paint over the area, and 3) follow with a coat of traditional gray paint. When a ship is resting in port, it is always a good time to chip and paint, and to undertake other small maintenance items.

There was a need to be careful and thorough in everything I did. For instance, the term "holiday" was something to be avoided. If upon completing a paint job someone noted a small unpainted area mistakenly overlooked, the name "holiday" was given to it. Having too many holidays was not a good idea, since the penalty was a "bad look" and/or a judgment of laziness.

By the second or third day, I had acquired a nickname: "gadget." The name pleased the Bos'n and didn't bother me because it seemed easier to avoid "Midshipman" or "Cadet," especially since the deck crew appreciated how green I was about these new and various shipboard chores. Besides, there wasn't much I could do about it.

It was not long before the *Catoche* was fully loaded. The stevedores had finished returning the booms to their births, and we were ready to depart. In the meantime, one additional deck cadet returned, Burdette Otis; he still had remaining sea time to serve before heading back to the Academy, which for him required one more voyage. I remember him telling me the not-so-good news that the Chief Mate, who had come up in the ranks through the "hawse pipe," didn't much care for "schoolship cadets." Then, I was again pleasantly surprised when two engine cadets, Frank McDonald and Bob Haines, also arrived prior to our putting out to sea. There was a certain camaraderie now inasmuch as we were about the same age and "were in the same boat together."

Our cabin contained a porthole, two double-decker beds with pull-out drawers below the beds, four standing lockers, and probably a sink. A salt-water shower was a short walk down the passageway.

The Golden Gate Bridge and the Blue Pacific
The time for departure had arrived, the ship was fully loaded, and the good ship SS *Cape Catoche* and all aboard were ready to sail for "somewhere in the Pacific."

The mooring lines holding the *Catoche* to the pier were let go; the ship's whistle signaled that we were going to leave the dock; the engine below decks sprang into action; and we began to move "slow ahead," although no one knew what our exact destination would be—not even the Captain, who had been directed not to open the orders until the *Catoche* was well clear of land.

It was exciting to hear the ship's whistle blow, and it was impressively louder than I expected. I had seen the Golden Gate Bridge from afar, but now at cruising speed we were suddenly passing below it—quite an inspiring sight! The Pacific Ocean's beautiful deep blue color surprised me as I had grown up on the Atlantic coast where the ocean was more a green color, and not as beautiful. Yet, I noted a certain sense of being "woozy" at this time due to the turbulence of the tides running under the Golden Gate Bridge, causing the *Catoche* to roll about. For several moments I struggled with the thought: "Don't tell me that I'm going to be a candidate for seasickness!" Fortunately as we moved away from the bridge and farther off shore, the unsettling feeling in my stomach disappeared, and I managed to escape seasickness for the remainder of my sea time.

As the *Catoche* continued moving forward, I noted that land on both the starboard and the port side of the *Catoche* was peeling away from us. It was as if the land was thus opening its arms wide, much like a huge gate allowing us to proceed to the wide and beckoning ocean. Standing on the bridge, I felt a refreshing cool breeze as the landscape gradually receded from view.

The *Catoche* was soon surrounded by ocean on all sides as she steamed ahead on course. It was time for the Captain to open our orders. Our first stop was to be Pearl Harbor. It was now early summer in 1944.

Routine Duties at Sea

The day-time chores were listed by the Chief Mate, passed down to the Bos'n and from him on to the rest of the crew, which included the deck cadets. The seamen were fine to work with and were professional for the most part, and the Navy Armed Guard personnel on board managed the guns under the supervision of Navy Lieutenant Ford.

In addition to a variety of painting chores, aforementioned, other details included sweeping and cleaning decks and passageways, shining brass, greasing the winches and wire for the booms, and the like.

I would often wander to the fantail (open deck at the stern of a vessel) after work, and join Armed Guard sailors exercising with some home-made weights, so that we could attempt to stay in shape after hours. One barbell (a metal bar attached to two cans of cement) weighed 100 pounds. When the fantail was moving upward under the motion of the ocean swells, the barbell was quite light, but when the fantail was moving in a downward direction, it was another story entirely.

When the alarm went off and we heard "General Quarters" over the ship's loudspeaker, everyone immediately responded to a previously assigned gun station. I was a loader for a Navy Armed Guard sailor who was strapped to a 20mm machine gun and did the shooting as long as he was able. We both were located within one of the eight chest-high, steel-gun tubs,[8] and we wore helmets and life jackets. I was surprised how heavy the loaded magazines were—surely more than 65 lbs.—that had to be lifted to shoulder height. The *Catoche* had the armaments of a mini-battleship since

---

[8] A gun tub is a steel circular tub reaching about chest high, which served as a source of protection from enemy gunfire. Each tub contained a 20mm machine

she was fitted with a 3-inch/50 caliber cannon on the bow and a 5-inch/38 caliber cannon on the fantail. I later noted that when the cannon on the fantail fired, the whole stern appeared to jump up due to the recoil of the heavy weapon.

Also, at "General Quarters" a Navy signalman, who was appropriately named "Flags," worked the blinker light and was in charge of the signal flags on the bridge. Navy Lieutenant Ford, who was in charge of the U.S. Navy Armed Guard personnel, was also stationed on the bridge as was the ship's captain and one or two other of the ship's officers.

We also had quite a bit of instruction on small-boat handling at the Academy and spent a night in a life boat during our time as plebes. Lifeboat drills were mandatory and involved all crew on board the *Catoche* to report to their pre-assigned lifeboat wearing their life jackets. These drills were required at least once per trip.

After daytime chores, I spent a significant amount of time working on the monster "Sea Project." This project required a detailed knowledge of virtually every aspect that goes into enabling a ship to function—from a future deck officer's point of view. This meant becoming familiar with the equipment both within the ship's wheelhouse as well as on the deck. The project included a large number of questions that pertained to such things as navigation, signaling, gunnery, loading and discharging supplies, docking and undocking procedures, ship construction, and Rules of the Road, to name a few. When not working on the project, I often spent one or two evenings on the bridge.

Before meals we used the salt water showers to wash off the accumulated paint, polish, and grease, in order to be more presentable in the officers' dining room. Somehow I remember powdered eggs and powdered milk being consistently on the menu.

Docking Procedures

During the docking process or leaving port, the deck cadet on the bridge could observe first-hand the procedures, as well as the tech-

---

gun that was mainly used against incoming enemy planes. A Navy gunner did all the shooting as long as he was able. Lifeboat equipment and supplies were also checked regularly. We had lifeboat drills as well as gunnery practice at sea.

Fig. 8. Tying up lines. (Source: *Midships, 1946,* United States Merchant Marine Academy, Kings Point).

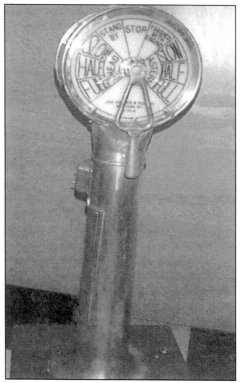

Fig 9. Wheelhouse engine telegraph. (Source: U S. Merchant Marine Academy Museum.)

nique of dropping and raising the anchor, the mechanics of working the cargo booms, docking and undocking procedures, and tying up lines, i.e., all the different lines and the order in which they are tied and/or stowed (Fig. 8). Other items to be learned included the selection of the proper signal flags and what they meant, the technique of opening and closing hatches, and recording water depth by sonar when maneuvering within a channel or shallow water. I was often assigned to relay the orders given by the Pilot or captain using the ship's telegraph on the bridge, which was connected to the engine room telegraph by moving the handles to relay information such as "Stop, Slow Ahead, Slow Astern, Full Ahead," and so on (Fig. 9).

Also, during docking procedures, the Chief Mate was in charge of the bow lines and the Third Mate was in charge of the after (stern) lines, while the Second Mate remained on the bridge along with the Captain. The Captain would not use a megaphone during the docking procedure (he didn't need it). It did my heart good to see the Chief Mate jump straight up in the air when the Captain, standing on the bridge, would bellow in a booming voice directed towards him: "Let go the g-d bow lines!" It was a pleasant pay-back for us cadets.

Pl. 5

On occasion when the ship was entering or leaving unfamiliar ports, a Pilot was needed and would often come on board. He was very familiar with the waterways, ocean currents, winds, navigational aids, docking facilities, and possible need for tugs. He would generally take over the duties of navigating the ship as it slowly found its way to the dock, or when leaving the dock, as the ship headed out to sea. Tug boats were sometimes used for extra help in maneuvering in and out of port.

Flag Codes

Pl. 6

The international code flag "H" (named "How" but really stands for "Have Pilot") would be flown from the yardarm at these times. This is still flown today in every port over the globe. There are code flags for all the letters of the alphabet from A to Z. When flown alone, each flag had a distinct message. Also, each ship can be identified by its four code flags flying vertically from the yardarm. This is illustrated by the four identification flags flying from the ship's yardarm. The photo shows these code flags by the letters, which spelled a ship's identification: N.S.N.H.

The flag that stands for "B" (referred to as Baker) is flown when taking on fuel or ammunition or other flammable materials. It was also flown during my second trip in Redwood City, California, when loading all five holds of the SS *Catoche* with drums of 100-octane (then known as high-octane) gasoline.

Pearl Harbor

As we steamed into the harbor in July 1944, I tried to imagine what the Navy base had looked like before the Japanese attack on December 7, 1941. It occurred to me that in pre-war days Hawaii must have been prime shore duty.

When we arrived, there were still signs of continuing repairs in Pearl Harbor, but a salvage operation, considered one of history's greatest, had been accomplished. Most of the work took place in the Pearl Harbor Navy Yard. By February 1942, the battleships *Pennsylvania*, *Maryland*, and *Tennessee* as well as the cruisers *Honolulu*, *Helena*, and *Raleigh* and several smaller-size vessels had been put back into service or in good enough condition to reach the mainland for final repairs. Also the battleships *Nevada*, *California*, and *West Virginia* were re-floated and, following significant repairs, were returned to service.

At the time of attack, the battleship *Arizona* sank at her moorings when a bomb detonated the ammunition magazine and blew the bow wide open. Her superstructure remained above the water line for some years until it was finally cut away after the war. The USS *Arizona* Memorial commemorates the events of December 7. The Memorial now rests atop the original weather deck. Incidentally, the USS *Missouri*, on whose deck the Japanese signed the surrender to the Allied Powers in Tokyo bay on September 2, 1945, is moored directly ahead of the USS *Arizona*, a glorious sight to behold—the beginning and end of World War II in the Pacific.

In December 1943, two years after the attack, the capsized battleship *Oklahoma* was righted during salvaging operations by attaching numerous cables to Ford Island and winching her into an upright position while still flooded. Thereafter, 400 bodies were recovered, of which only 35 could be identified. Under tow to the West Coast in May 1947, the USS *Oklahoma* sank and was lost forever.

So, when we arrived at Pearl in 1944, the clean-up effort was almost totally complete. Honolulu and its surroundings appeared to be untouched. I remember visiting the Royal Hawaiian Hotel, which was evidently being used as an R & R (Rest and Recreation) base for submariners in the summer of 1944. Beautiful Waikiki beach was covered with barbed wire, so no one was in the water.

Sailors were everywhere in Honolulu. I was embarrassed when I received salutes from sailors who noted the thin gold braid on my midshipman's hat. Undoubtedly the sailors were trained to salute anyone with any type of gold braid.

I tasted my first beer in the Hickam Field Officer's Club in Hawaii, having been invited to do so by some of the ship's officers. I briefly felt like a "big shot," but the beer tasted awful!

After a few days of loading supplies and fuel, the *Catoche* left Pearl Harbor and began an almost holiday trip to various beautiful Pacific islands.

Crossing the Equator

The good ship *Catoche* crossed the Equator on August 4, 1944. I had never heard about the ancient custom of being welcomed to King Neptune's realm by way of a special "celebration." Tradition holds that those sailors who had never crossed the equator were known as "pollywogs." After crossing, and following the ritual, sailors were then known as "shellbacks."

Summoned by a "sheriff" to King Neptune's court, we were advised by a bailiff of certain charges relating to inadequacies of our behavior. Several members of the court then testified to the offensive behavior of the pollywog before it. The court pronounced sentence and a barber coated our hair with grease. Then, I remember being blindfolded and wearing only skivvies and walking barefoot in single file along a wet, wooden boardwalk (catwalk) on the deck, along with a few other men. The catwalk was conveniently doused from the ocean's spray since the ship was loaded down nearly to the water level. This served as an ideal medium for permitting small electric shocks to be delivered to both feet, thanks to a very creative electrician on board. Having survived this, each of us was sequentially covered from head to toe with a mixture of red lead paint and mustard. Still blindfolded, we were told that we were to be pushed backwards overboard into the ocean (perhaps to be introduced to Davey Jones?). Being a swimmer, that thought didn't bother me too much. Someone gave me a shove, and I fell backwards, landing with a large splash in the water. The blindfold fell off, and I found myself in a huge tarpaulin filled to the brim with sea water. This was the grand finale. In the end, we had all crossed the Equator! A few days later, each of us was presented with a large certificate attesting to the ceremony, which I still have

Pl. 7

framed, noting the date, the location, and the name of the vessel, along with Captain Sanders' signature! We were also given a wallet-size card attesting to our transformation to shellbacks. I kept my card handy since I didn't relish a repeat performance should I be transferred to another ship in the future!

I should mention that the Bos'n was the director of the court and other members included King Neptune along with witnesses and onlookers. A "salty" cadet, Otis, played the role of a mermaid, having crossed on an earlier trip, and was now one of the members of King Neptune's court. Otis was a nice looking guy, with hardly a beard, who looked quite fetching with lipstick and a blond wig. It had been several weeks since anyone had seen a "blond." Sensing he had caught the eye of the Bos'n at the conclusion of the event, he rushed to his cabin, took off the lipstick, removed the wig, and quickly put on his working clothes.

Beautiful Islands

One of our early ports was Pago Pago, an island belonging to American Samoa. We then proceeded to Funafuti, a small Commonwealth colony. The next port was the gem of all the islands in my view: It was Bora Bora, a member of the Polynesian Islands and labeled by many as the "Queen of the Pacific." The *Catoche* then proceeded to Suva, the capital of the Fiji Islands, and lastly, Noumea, New Caledonia. At each island, supplies and mail were delivered.

The island of Bora Bora was special. Approaching the island I   Pl. 8
noticed the lush green mountains rising up from the blue Pacific Ocean. As the ship drew near, white sandy beaches came into view. The depth of the water varied enough to present striking shades of blue and green. Palm trees lined the beaches. I remember thinking: This is the nearest thing to a get-away paradise, a great place to visit in peacetime. Bora Bora is known for its beautiful lagoon, which encouraged the author, James Michener, to label it "the most beautiful lagoon in the world." People there spoke French, and while taking a brief walk after we had docked, I passed an office building on the main street, and glancing towards the back of

the structure, I spied a strange sight—a tennis court. This brought a warm feeling into my heart; it was nice to see that tennis was still being played—at least somewhere in the Pacific during wartime.

Noumea, New Caledonia, was the last port of call. It was the third largest island in the Pacific after New Guinea and New Zealand, and is located between Australia and the Fiji Islands. Some believe it is an unspoiled French "secret." Our time in port, as in all the above ports, was limited to only a few days. Noumea did not impress me in 1944 and seemed to lack the beauty of the other islands. It was a dirty port, and the little I saw didn't beckon. Most likely, the more attractive areas were on the other side of the island.

When reading one of the many of the letters my mother had saved, I mentioned going for a short walk when ashore in Noumea. A Navy lieutenant accompanied by three sailors wearing arm bands with the Shore Patrol (SP) insignia approached me. I wondered if I had committed some sort of crime. The officer said "Hello" and laughed, and went on to say, "I knew you were a cadet as soon as I saw the gray paint behind your ear." He had recently graduated from Kings Point. We enjoyed a brief visit.

I soon became accustomed to the whole routine of work, study, lifeboat drills, gunnery practice, and lifting weights on the fantail with some of the Navy crew.

This first trip was largely uneventful. Gunnery practice was always exciting, as was my first view of flying fish, and a few squalls. These beautiful islands, the most beautiful in the Pacific Ocean, were spared from conflict, and after discharging all our supplies, we headed back to the West Coast.

Second Voyage (1944–1945)

The ship tied up at Redwood City, California. Within days, we were taking on drums of 100-octane gasoline. The barrels were stacked up and secured in each of the ship's five holds. When all the drums were loaded on board and the hatches secured, trucks and other military vehicles were lashed down on top of the hatches. (The space on deck alongside the secured hatches was taken up by an assortment of military equipment as well.) The ship's carpenter made an elevated wooden catwalk to enable the crew to go from the bow to the stern. At this time, the ship was heavily loaded with cargo, and the waterline was once again very close to the ship's main deck.

When passing under the Golden Gate Bridge, and heading west once more, I sensed that this trip would be different. The Captain again waited until we were out to sea before opening the orders. The word was that we were eventually heading for Saipan by way of Pearl Harbor and Eniwetok. We didn't spend much time in Pearl Harbor other than for refueling. We now set course for Eniwetok. The drums of high-octane gasoline were needed by our B-29 bombers that were beginning to arrive at a hastily built airfield on Saipan. The airfield would allow our bombers to fly closer to nearby Japanese-held islands and, in the long run, would be another "stepping stone" nearer to the Japanese mainland.

Before heading for Saipan, we first met up with an overwhelming number of ships anchored off the coast of Eniwetok. This was the staging area where a number of convoys would be parceled out. I can still see the Captain standing on the bridge as we approached the atoll. He was so excited, much like a little boy, as he jumped up and down and shouted, "I have never seen so many g-d ships in one place in my whole life!" From one horizon to the other, the entire area was blanketed with ships. All were loaded down, and their decks, like ours, undoubtedly appeared to be only a few inches above the water line. Many of them also had tanks and other military vehicles lashed to the decks. The rumor was that the majority of these vessels were to be involved in the in-

vasion of the Philippines. This sounded exciting to me, and being a
naïve young teenager, I was somewhat disappointed to learn our
orders had not changed; we were to proceed to Saipan.

Referring to the charts on board, I noted that the Mariana Islands were composed of a series of islands arranged as a chain going
from north to south. Saipan was the northernmost of the four islands. The other three, going in a southern direction, were Tinian,
Rota, and Guam. The island of Saipan was 1,200 miles from Tokyo, but its importance was highlighted as a stepping stone to the
Japanese homeland.

A half-dozen supply ships made up our small convoy. Two
small Navy patrol vessels (Fig. 10) served as our "guardians." In
heavy seas, we lost sight of the patrol vessels as they sank down in
the trough of a wave, only to reappear at the crest of the following
wave. Despite wartime conditions, the daily routine aboard ship
continued with routine gunnery practice, painting, polishing, cleaning the decks, and checking lifeboat equipment. The captain and
deck officer were vigilant to keep *Catoche* "on station" within the
convoy group.

All ships were given the same coded "zigzag pattern," to be
done in unison; this was, in theory, to frustrate Japanese submarines hidden below the surface. In order to do this, I recall that a
zig-zag template was superimposed upon the gyro compass for
steering and thus directing the new course to be followed by the
helmsman, either to port or starboard, for a predetermined time
(perhaps 20 minutes or so) before returning back to the normal
course once more. There were various patterns of course deviations
and timed intervals to choose from; one set was chosen by all the
ships before the convoy set out (Fig. 11). A leading ship in the convoy was labeled the "Commodore." When this vessel made a predetermined zig-zag change, to port or starboard, all the remaining
ships in the convoy immediately followed suit.

The Captain's cabin opened on to a small deck, a level just
below the flying bridge where, on occasion, he might venture forth
and sit in the sun. I was assigned an extra job of daily sweeping
and swabbing down the Captain's small private deck. One day,
while sitting in his chair, he silently watched me carry out this

Fig. 10. Patrol vessel in heavy seas. (Source: National Archives, Washington, D.C.)

Fig. 11. Convoy underway. (Courtesy: The Mariners' Museum, Newport News, VA.)

routine. Waiting until I completed the task and had coiled the hose back up, placing it on a bracket on the ship's bulkhead, he suddenly yelled at the top of his Estonian voice, "Cadet!" He followed this with a series of unmentionable epithets while pointing to a piece of paper about the size of a paper match, which I had missed. Without mentioning all the words in his outburst, the gist was: "If you're going to do anything in life, do it well, g-d it, or don't do it at all!" By reflex, I rapidly retrieved the tiny paper and simultaneously jammed that lesson into my head where it resides permanently to this day!

Nighttime brought an entirely different ambiance for all on board. As the ship was blacked out, this enabled the engine room personnel to "blow the tubes" (so that less black smoke would be emitted from the stack during the day), thus decreasing the *Catoche*'s visibility to Japanese ships, subs, and planes. In order to go on deck, we were required to pass through a series of black drapes hanging inside the passageways leading to the exits, which were lit with red lights. White lights are more easily seen across the water. Smoking was strictly forbidden.

Fig. 12. Immersion rubber suit. (Source: National Archives.)

We were issued whole body immersion rubber suits (Fig. 12) in the event we should be blown into the water from a torpedo, aircraft, enemy surface vessel, or a mine. The idea crept into my mind that exploding drums of gasoline would give me very little time to run to my room and put on the rubber suit. Years later, during back-yard cookouts while spraying the charcoal with lighter fluid, I reflected on just how cavalier we were at the time, living side by side with seemingly endless drums of gasoline containing the potential for a cataclysmic explosion. Today I would be more cautious (although "nervous" might be a better word).

It is amazing that I experienced at the time a naïve sense of security while working as a deck cadet, rather than being below decks in the engine room.[9] With a swimming background, I believed that, should I wind up in the "drink," I would at least be able to float. It occurred to me that the suits might keep the sailors a bit warmer when torpedoed in the frigid North Atlantic during the Murmansk run.

By the end of our abbreviated plebe time, and before shipping out, we had some additional training: Each of us had to jump from a high board into a swimming pool containing flames of burning oil. The trick was to splash the fire away with our hands while keeping the rest of our bodies underwater. This created a space through which we could then raise up our heads and look around. This seemed quite easy to me at the time. It was a good thing to experience even in a limited way, but especially instructive for those serving on tankers, ammunition ships, or ships like ours.

Although life at sea had more than its share of serious times, we had some amusing times as well. The Bos'n had pilfered some 3% beer that he on occasion offered me, unaware that I had not yet acquired a taste for beer. He called it "Australian beer" since there was no place to cool it without being discovered, and the beer was warm.

Toward the end of six months at sea, rumor had it that a few of the crew began drinking "Jungle juice"—a mixture of methyl alcohol and fruit juice that I later found out could lead to blindness. There was a story of an unknown crewman from another ship who drank the alcohol out of the ship's compass. (I'm not sure this was really true.)

One night near the equator, while I was speaking with the Second Officer, who was on watch, the Lookout sailor stationed on the bow telephoned the bridge and reported a white light two points off the port bow. The Second Officer, who also served as the ship's official navigator, replied, "That is SIRIUS," prompting the Lookout to sound the alarm for "General Quarters!" The embarrassed Second Officer, greatly humiliated, quickly announced "Cancel General Quarters!" The sailor hadn't realized that it wasn't really SERIOUS; it was SIRIUS, the brightest star in the sky!

---

[9] Post-war statistics found that the loss of life was virtually the same whether one was on deck or in the engine room when a ship was attacked.

Saipan

The invasion of the island of Saipan began on June 5, 1944. The capture of the island was important because air bases were essential for B-29 Superfortress bombers to launch attacks against Japan itself. The B-29 had a normal range of 2,850 miles. Loaded with bombs, a B-29 traveling at 358 mph was just able to reach Japan from the Mariana Islands and return safely.

We arrived at Saipan in the fall of 1944, greeted by bodies of dead Japanese soldiers, bloated, waterlogged, and washed up on the beach adjacent to the pier where we tied up. There were many caves on the island and a significant number of Japanese soldiers were still resisting. The caves made good bunkers. Rather than surrendering, many of the Japanese soldiers and civilians jumped from the high cliffs and perished among the rocks and in the water below.

While the drums of gasoline were being off-loaded from the ship, another cadet and I spotted a disabled Japanese tank standing in the middle of a field nearby. We decided to stretch our legs and to examine it. No sooner had we arrived at the tank than we heard several "pings"—bullets hitting the tank. We took off in a big hurry. In hindsight, standing alone in a field was a dumb thing to do.

Christmas Time 1944: The War Heats Up

By December 1944, the weather was very warm, around 90 degrees, and higher for those in the engine room, and the mail finally caught up with us. Families and loved ones of course never knew where our ship had gone, since all our letters were censored. Since my father had died when he was 41, and I was 11 years old (June 6 was our common birthday), a mother's first instinct, of course, is to make sure her only child is at least warm, although she never realized where we were located. So I smiled when I opened my mother's Christmas present: *winter underwear.* An uncle had sent a pipe, although I had never smoked and still have never picked up the habit. It seemed so ironic to listen to Bing Crosby sing, "I'm Dreaming of a White Christmas," sent short wave, courtesy of the

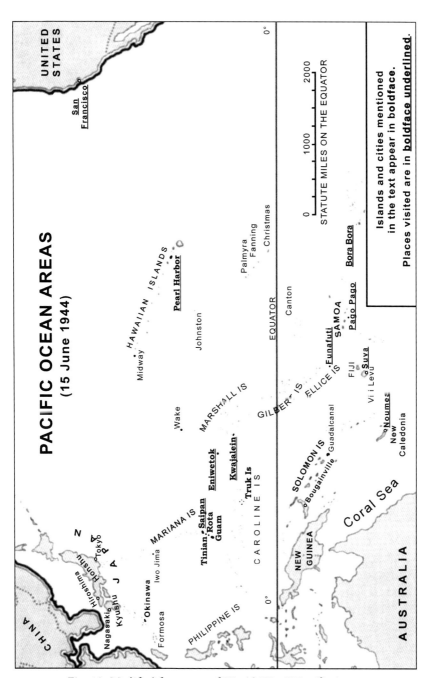

Fig. 13: Modified from map of World War II Pacific Areas.

legendary Japanese propagandist, Tokyo Rose. Between songs she would try to induce all U.S. forces to surrender.

A few nights later under a full moon, Japanese bombers were overhead bombing the B-29 air base close by the dock where we were tied up. A follow-up attack occurred the next night. Fortunately, our ship escaped unscathed both times. The night sky was filled with tracers from ground fire and would rival today's Macy's Fourth of July fireworks; some of the Japanese bombers were struck and crashed into the water around us. A couple of pilots were able to parachute, and were caught in our searchlights as they descended into the water; I'll never know what happened to them. Smoke screen canisters were lit by all the ships in an attempt to provide cover for the area. Those few action-filled days were both frightening and exciting.

Earlier Beginnings of the "Stepping Stone" Strategy

Back on April 18, 1942, Lieutenant Colonel Jimmy Doolittle led a flight of 16 Army B-25 bombers, launched from the deck of the aircraft carrier, USS *Hornet*, on a raid on Japan's home islands. It was a one-way trip. Doolittle bailed out over China and was rescued. For this daring feat, he was promoted to Brigadier General and received the Medal of Honor. Although all the bombers delivered their load of bombs onto Tokyo, no significant military damage was inflicted. Ultimately, the raid served primarily as a morale builder for America at that time.

Saipan was still quite a distance from Tokyo. (See Map, page 39.) Because our forces had captured Eniwetok and Kwajalein in the Marshall Islands earlier that February, they were subsequently able to invade Saipan in June, and Guam in July 1944. This was an example of the "stepping stone" strategy that our government was pursuing at that time. In October 1944, American B-29 bombers took off from Guam to finish off the remaining forces on the Truk Islands situated in the Caroline Islands to the south. This cleared the southern area of potential threats so that the B-29 bases further to the north on the Marianas were secure, enabling them to make future attacks on the Philippines and ultimately on Japan's homeland.

The Plan for the Invasion of Japan: 1945 and 1946

Operation Olympic (the invasion of Kyushu) was targeted for November 1, 1945, and Operation Coronet, if all went well on Kyushu, would begin against Honshu on March 1, 1946.[10] Both operations would involve a staggering total of 4.5 million American servicemen! Fortunately, both the United States and Japan were spared the potential of huge numbers of casualties when the war ended after atomic bombs were dropped on Hiroshima and Nagasaki.

The Introduction of the A-bomb

The B-29 bomber "Enola Gay," piloted by Lt. Col. Paul Tibbets, dropped a uranium bomb named "Little Boy" on the Japanese city of Hiroshima on the morning of August 6, 1945. Tibbets took off from the airbase on Tinian. Accompanying him was Major Charles Sweeny in his own bomber, the "Great Artiste," carrying measuring instruments that were dropped by parachute and transmitting pressure, heat, and radiation information from the explosion back to scientists aboard the aircraft.

Three days later, Major Charles Sweeney, this time piloting the B-29 bomber named "Bock's Car," took off from Tinian and dropped a plutonium bomb named "Fat Man," which was more powerful than the first A-bomb, on the city of Nagasaki. Low on fuel, Sweeny barely made it back to Okinawa. The combined destruction of both cities and loss of life was so massive that these explosions contributed to Japan's surrender to the Supreme Commander for the Allied Powers, General Douglas MacArthur, on September 2, 1945 onboard the USS *Missouri* in Tokyo Bay. Though more than 100,000 people died, and an additional 40,000 later died from radiation effects in those two cities, General George C. Marshall estimated that, had the invasion proceeded, up to a million United States casualties and perhaps even more Japanese casualties would have occurred. Virtually all American servicemen were overjoyed to see the war end.

---

[10] "Operation Downfall (US Invasion of Japan]: US Plans and Japanese Countermeasures," by D.M. Giangreco, US Army Command and General Staff College, February 16, 1998. Center for East Asian Studies, University of Kansas.

Highly classified information about the plans for the invasion of Japan, recently released from the National Archives, have now revealed that the United States had grossly underestimated the Japanese military, air, and sea power while invasion preparations were underway. In addition, Okinawa had become the staging area for the invasion. Many troops, ships, and equipment were in place, but when the war ended in September 1945, the "invasion forces" were disbanded. This fact increases in significance when it is pointed out that an unexpected typhoon (Typhoon Louise) struck Okinawa on October 9, 1945,[11] five weeks after the surrender of Japanese forces. Waves up to 40 feet high and winds clocked at 120 knots wreaked an enormous amount of destruction in its wake. Dozens of Americans died and 270 ships were sunk or severely damaged. Should Japan's surrender not have occurred, this unexpected storm would have added still more to the tragedy in the Pacific among the American troops in the staging areas.

The Role of the U.S. Merchant Marine Fleet in World War II

During the first four years of sea-war hostilities (1939–42), Allied shipping losses far exceeded the number of new ships being constructed by a factor of four to one. Beginning in 1943, new ship construction gradually began to outpace losses, which made the rapid deployment and support of Allied troops around the globe quicker and more substantial. In addition to conveying troops, the U.S. Merchant Marine ships delivered ammunition, tanks, bombs, fuel, airplanes, food, and raw materials in massive quantities, thus providing crucial support for the Allied invasions and occupation of enemy territory.[12] The role of the United States Merchant Marine in the war cannot be underestimated; indeed, it not only shortened the war, but made possible the Allied victory on land and sea.

In the aftermath of the war, the United States Merchant Marine returned prisoners from the armies of Japan and Germany, who had surrendered or been captured, back to their homelands.

---

[11] "Typhoons & Hurricanes: Pacific Typhoons at Okinawa, October 1945." Naval Historical Center, Washington, Navy Yard, Washington, D.C. (February 11, 1946).

[12] See www.usmm.org: "American Merchant Marine in World War II."

Likewise, we returned United States troops, as well as the wounded and the dead, back to the States, while moving occupation forces to the previous war zones. The Merchant Marine also played a crucial role in transferring refugees, who had been uprooted or would be exiled by ensuing conflicts as a result of the war, to their former homes and to new homes around the world.

The SS *Catoche* Returns Home

Having unloaded all the gasoline drums and vehicles, we received our orders to return to Pearl Harbor in early January 1945. We were now underway, traveling light with less cargo in the holds, which at times made us feel we were at a rodeo, or rather *in* a rodeo. Our *Catoche* rolled and pitched with the vengeance of a wild bull. While steaming toward Pearl harbor, we were about 100 miles north of a large typhoon. Large waves always arrive before a big storm actually hits. We learned that a Navy ship, possibly a destroyer, was hit by the brunt of a storm south of us and flipped over, with considerable loss of life. Though we were tossed around, we missed its full force.

Approaching Pearl Harbor at night time, a United States Navy patrol plane dropped flares and exposed our ship, thus making us a sitting duck for any submarine in the area. This occurred despite our warning the plane by blinker and radio that we were an American ship. When the Navy flyer failed to heed our communication, all hands were ordered to man the guns and shoot it down, but it suddenly veered off and left us. I never saw our Armed Guard Lieutenant become so angry. He reported the incident to the Naval Headquarters as soon as we docked.

Revisiting Pearl Harbor I realized this was our final stopover, for we were on the way back to the States. There was one vivid impression of Pearl remaining: An ocean-going tug was bringing back a badly damaged supply ship, which was markedly listing to port. Tears came to my eyes when all the ships, both at anchor and dock side, blew their ship's whistles in tribute to the gallant ship as she entered the harbor. Though badly wounded and beaten, she was still afloat.

Fig. 14. Kings Point Regiment standing at attention before a football game.
Fall, 1945. (Source: *Midships, 1946*, United States Merchant Marine Academy.)

Chapter 4:

Back to the Academy

In February of 1945, it was time to report back to the Academy for a year of advanced training, and now there were 4,912 cadets. This was to be an intensely busy time that eventually led to graduation, a Naval Reserve Commission, and a Coast Guard license. Our section graduated in March 1946, and we were one of the last of the "wartime accelerated" graduates.

As upper classmen, we could now pick on the plebes. Should a plebe fail to square a corner, for example, an upper classman spotting this would yell at him out of his dorm room, or any other spot on the campus, and make him go back and square it. The plebe always did it! We were still part of the regiment, and we had to abide by all the rules set forth by the institution. Most of us, however, were too busy to go out of our way to harass the plebes.

No more "camping out" on board the *Emory Rice!* We now occupied barracks—four of us in a dorm room, with one desk, four chairs, and two double-decker beds. Rifles were stored under each mattress, an exact number of bed springs from the head of the bed as well as a certain number of springs from the side of each bed. Taped bugle calls emanated through the Academy intercom loudspeaker: Reveille awoke us in the morning; taps allowed us to sleep at night. Announcements also were piped over the intercom proclaiming the "uniform of the day" as well as any other orders pertaining to the entire regiment. Before dressing, all the cadets were ordered to do setting-up exercises. Every hallway in all the barracks would then be jammed with a line of unenthusiastic and half-asleep cadets dressed only in their pajamas and a robe, doing these pesky exercises. The rooms were then cleaned up and subject to inspection daily by the cadet officers. All items of wear were assigned to special drawers.

Pl. 9

Fig. 15. Kings Point Regimental Dress Review, Saturday morning. (Source: *A Pictorial Review of Kings Point,* United States Merchant Marine Academy, n.d.)

Plate 1: Color Guard at Kings Point.
(Source: *Midships, 1946*, United States Merchant Marine Academy, Kings Point.)

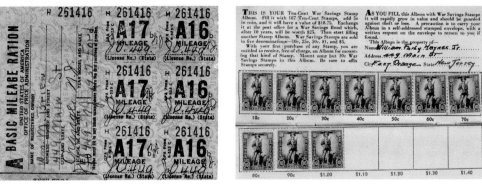

Plate 2:
Gasoline rationing stamps and War Savings stamp album.

Plate 3:
A variety of three-cent stamps
featuring the Coast Guard, Navy,
and Merchant Marine.

Plate 4: Cadet-Midshipman Edwin J. O'Hara. Painting by W.N. Wilson.
(Courtesy: United States Merchant Marine Academy Museum.)

Plate 5: Tugboat in icy waters entering Bremerhaven, Germany.

Plate 6:
Ship's four-code (identification) flags
plus flag "H" indicating "I have a pilot on board."

Plate 7: *Imperium Neptuni Regis*. Davey Jones certificate
commemorates crossing the Equator.

Plate 8: U.S. Navy ships in Teavanui Harbor, Bora Bora, February 1942
(Source: U.S. Navy photo: # 80-G-K-1117)

Plate 9: Kings Point cadet making up a bed.
(Source: *United States Merchant Marine Academy*, Harmony House, 1988.
Photo courtesy: Michael S. Yamashita.)

Plate 10: Kings Point marching band.
(Source: *United States Merchant Marine Academy*, Harmony House, 1988.
Photo courtesy: Michael S. Yamashita.)

Plate 11: Winners of the Superintendent's Cup. From left to right: Ulman, R.*; Ronnenburg, B.; Reilly, Tom; Dailey, E.; Matley, B.*; Riggin, C.*; Kulka, L.; Tartaglino, A.; Ballas, A.; Haynes, W. F.; and kneeling in front, McIntyre, M. (Coxswain)*.   * Deceased.

Plate 12: USS *General George M. Randall* medical staff.

Plate 13: USNS *General W.C. Langfitt* in dry dock, head-on.

Plate 14: USNS *General W.C. Langfitt*, awaiting the refugees.

Plate 15: Child coming on board the *Langfitt*.

Plate 16: Lifeboat drill aboard the *Langfitt*.

Plate 17: USNS *General W.C. Langfitt* commander on deck.

Plate 18: Sailors returning from shore leave.

Plate 19: Children's Christmas party, with Santa, in Bremerhaven.

Plate 20: USNS *Pvt. Elden H. Johnson* docked, with band playing on shore.

Plate 21: USNS *Pvt. Elden H. Johnson* in the locks of the Panama Canal.
The pilot is sitting on the "flying bridge."

Plate 22: USNS *Geiger*, view of the bow with troops on deck.

Plate 23: White Cliffs of Dover, England.

Plate 24: Pilot boarding the *Geiger*.

Plate 25: Waves breaking over the bow of the *Geiger*.
See the dark figure on the deck, under the wave.

Plate 26: Raft crossing the Atlantic, west to east. A strange sight.

Plate 27: The *Geiger* at sea in heavy weather.

Plate 28: Sunset over the Atlantic from the *Geiger*.
The end of the day. The end of Sea Time.

You never enjoy the world aright, till the sea itself
Floweth in your veins, till you are clothed with the
Heavens, and crowned with the stars: and perceive
Yourself to be the sole heir of the whole world.

Centuries of Meditations (I, 29, 30)
Thomas Traherne (English Mystic, ca. 1673–74)

Saturday was the day when the inspection of rooms was especially thorough. As the inspection party entered the room, we would come to attention. We wore our dress uniforms at this time because there was always a formal review, unless the weather demanded a different outfit. (Before inspection, the floor would be waxed and highly buffed in order to see one's reflection.) The bed sheets were so tight that one could bounce a quarter on them, and the sheets were tucked at the corners in a special manner. This would be followed by a white-glove inspection (and pity the room occupants when the cadet officer noted dust on his nice white gloves after passing his hand over the transom or even the handle of the latrine). Failing the white-glove inspection would involve putting those responsible "on report," meaning that they would be doing some sort of extra duty. Regimental Dress Review (Fig. 15) on Saturday morning soon followed the inspection. The company voted the best in marching received a few extra hours for weekend liberty.

For the other days of the work week, Morning Colors took place at 8 o'clock. We stood in formation by companies while the Pl. 10 flag was raised and the band played the national anthem. There were 18 companies and three battalions that composed the regiment at this time, excluding those who were at sea. (I belonged to the 13th company of the 3rd battalion.) After Colors, we would then march in columns of two to our various classes. When the instructor arrived in class, the order was given by the section leader to come to attention.

I had the opportunity to be a member of the Academy swim team, which also allowed me to compete against various colleges on the East Coast; swimming thus served as a break in the daily routine so that I could enjoy a brief stint of "freedom." In hindsight, the Academy left nothing to chance—the time of boarding the bus, time of the meet, and time due back at the Academy. In today's world, this could be likened to being tracked by a modern spy satellite.

Another "breathing spell" occurred. Our lifeboat, represent- Pl. 11 ing the 13th company, won the Superintendent's Cup in the annual regimental lifeboat race at Kings Point (Fig. 16). This en-

Fig. 16. Throwing the coxswain overboard from the whale boat after winning the crew race for the Superintendent's Cup on Long Island Sound.

Fig. 17. Swan boat outing in Boston lagoon.

titled eleven of us, as the crew, to race against the Massachusetts Maritime Academy. We traveled to Boston by way of the Kings Point training ship SS *Gresham*, but the war ended in Europe (V-E Day) when we reached Boston, and the race was cancelled. We did, however, enjoy a free day and one of the events consisted of touring around a lake in the center of Boston aboard boats that contained the figure of a large swan on the stern. We were somewhat embarrassed when we saw a photograph of ourselves—in a Boston newspaper the very next day—sitting in the swan boats in our dress blues (Fig. 17).

In the fall of 1945, I was interviewed by the senior cadet officers for possible advancement as a cadet officer. Upon entering the room, the protocol was to snap to attention, flip your hat under your left arm, and sound off your name before starting the meeting. In the process of doing this, I snapped to attention and flipped my hat, which somehow sailed across the room. The interview proved to be rather short. I wasn't sure I wanted to be a cadet officer anyway.

Graduation from USMMA, March 1946

After a very busy year in this accelerated program, graduation day finally arrived on March 16, 1946. The war had ended. There were now 3,746 cadets in the regiment. Our section of 15 cadets, along with cadets from other sections, took the oath as Ensigns (Fig. 18) in the Naval Reserve of the United States Navy, and we received our United States Coast Guard Third Mate or Third Assistant Engineer licenses (Fig. 19), respectively. My license, a Third Mate's License, stated that I "can be intrusted to perform the duties of Third Mate on Steam and Motor Vessels of any gross tons, upon the waters of any ocean." These words seemed quite awesome to this newly minted young officer.

Now, the time spent in class was to be replaced by time at sea, as an officer. Along with that would come increased responsibility.

The first undergraduate who saluted any of us wearing our new officer's uniforms, by tradition, received one dollar (Fig. 20). I was more than happy to part with this currency, although as will

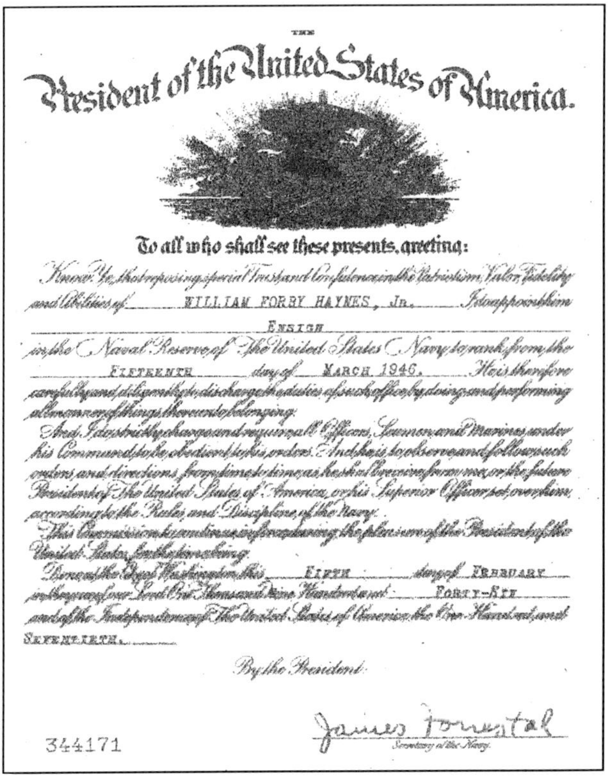
THE

President of the United States of America.

To all who shall see these presents, greeting:

Know Ye, that reposing special Trust and Confidence in the Patriotism, Valor, Fidelity and Abilities of WILLIAM FORRY HAYNES, Jr. I do appoint him ENSIGN in the Naval Reserve of The United States Navy to rank from the FIFTEENTH day of MARCH 1946. He is therefore carefully and diligently to discharge the duties of such office by doing and performing all manner of things thereunto belonging.

And I do strictly charge and require all Officers, Seamen and Marines under his Command to be obedient to his orders. And he is to observe and follow such orders and directions, from time to time, as he shall receive from me, or the future President of The United States of America, or his Superior Officer set over him, according to the Rules and Discipline of the Navy.

This Commission to continue in force during the pleasure of the President of the United States for the time being.

Done at the City of Washington this FIFTH day of FEBRUARY in the year of our Lord One Thousand Nine Hundred and FORTY-SIX and of the Independence of The United States of America the One Hundred and SEVENTIETH.

By the President:

James Forrestal
Secretary of the Navy.

344171

Fig. 18. Ensign commission from the Naval Reserve of the United States.

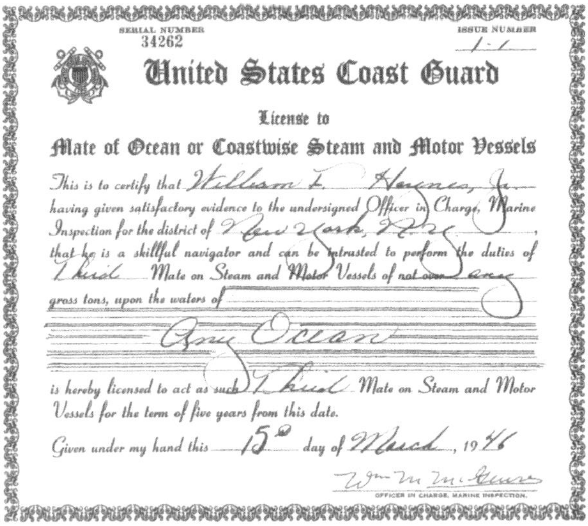
SERIAL NUMBER 34262

ISSUE NUMBER 1-1

United States Coast Guard

License to

Mate of Ocean or Coastwise Steam and Motor Vessels

This is to certify that William F. Haynes, Jr. having given satisfactory evidence to the undersigned Officer in Charge, Marine Inspection for the district of New York, N.Y., that he is a skillful navigator and can be intrusted to perform the duties of Third Mate on Steam and Motor Vessels of any gross tons, upon the waters of Any Ocean is hereby licensed to act as such Third Mate on Steam and Motor Vessels for the term of five years from this date.

Given under my hand this 15th day of March, 1946

Wm M. McGeuse
OFFICER IN CHARGE, MARINE INSPECTION.

Fig. 19. United States Coast Guard Third Mate's License.

Fig. 20. Saluting a new Ensign. (Source: *Midships, 1946*, United States Merchant Marine Academy.)

be shown in the rhyme below, I was somehow known to be thrifty. Prior to graduation, each of us in our section (C373) had written a poem about a fellow classmate. The author of the "work" was kept anonymous. I never did learn who penned this "ditty" and feel somewhat uneasy about sharing this poem, but I did laugh upon reading it again after all these years:

To William Forby Haynes, Jr.
It's a good thing you're a swimmer
For 'twill occupy your time
And furnish hours of pleasure
But never cost a dime.

Now Forby Boy, why don't you quit
And join the "Civie Frat"?
For that's the place to save the dough,
Just never wear a hat.

And so to help you live your life,
The kind you think the best,
Just spend the dough you think you need,
In here, put all the rest.

Don't let the boys give you a ride
Not just because you're thrifty,
Just take your bank each month, and go
Deposit the $59.50.

The year book showed each member in his dress uniform along with some comments below each name. Next to my picture (Fig. 21) was a brief biographical summary:

Varsity Swimming Team—Rowing Team, Championship. Aside from the fact that Bill has depleted the Academy's supply of piers, and small boats by repeated "attacks" on the waterfront, he has contributed his excellent back-stroke swimming ability to the Academy's Swimming Team. He was a member of the Regimental Rowing Crew which captured the Superintendent's Cup. Stubborn, he avoided controversial discussions, and exhibited a great sense of humor.

Fig. 21. Graduation photo: Cadet Midshipman
William F. Haynes, age 19. (Source: *Midships,
1946*, United States Merchant Marine Academy.)

My comment on the previous remark regarding my depleting
"the Academy's supply of piers": Instead of using a rudder when
steering those bulky whale boats, we were required to stand up in
the stern using a long sweep oar (Fig. 16). I found this to be a
clumsy way to steer the boat, and, needless to say, I had trouble
gliding alongside the pier. More often than not, it was bow first,
not a pretty sight.

Fig. 22. SS *Maritime Victory*. The first Victory (SS *American Victory*) was launched in June 1945. The Victory's length was 455 feet and the beam 62 feet, with a draft of 28 feet 6 inches. The engine was an Allis-Chalmers marine steam turbine with 6,000 hp driving a single propeller with a diameter of 18 feet 3 inches. The ship had a maximum cruising range of 23,500 miles. Victory ships had five internal holds and carried a maximum of 9,000 tons of cargo. Cape ships and Victory ships had the same armament, which is to say: one 3-inch/50-caliber cannon located on the bow, and a 5-inch/38-caliber cannon on the stern or fantail. There were six or eight 20mm machine guns located in separate gun tubs around the ship's midsection. The usual manpower consisted of a combination of 62 U.S. Merchant Marine seamen and about 25 U.S. Navy Armed Guard personnel. (Source: U.S. Government photo.)

Chapter 5:

SS *Maritime Victory* (1946)

Following graduation, and after spending ten days of R&R (Rest and Recreation) at home, I signed on as Third Mate for the SS *Maritime Victory* (Fig. 22). The Victory ship, which was the successor to the Liberty ship, began to replace the Liberty as the war drew to a close and provided significant additional capability to transport matériel. Liberty ships and other types of cargo ships and tankers played an indispensable role in World War II transporting troops, ammunition, and supplies to all theaters of war. It may be useful here to distinguish between a Liberty ship and a Victory ship.

The "Old" Liberty Ship
In September 1941, the first of 14 "Emergency" vessels was launched to support the defense of England. The first of these vessels was named SS *Patrick Henry*. In President Franklin D. Roosevelt's remarks at the launch ceremony, he cited Patrick Henry's 1775 speech that ended with: "Give me liberty or give me death." Roosevelt declared that this new class of ships would bring liberty to Europe, which gave rise thereafter to the name Liberty ship.

There were 2,710 mass-produced Liberty ships (Fig. 23) built in U.S. shipyards before and during World War II. Each one required about seven to ten days to build, and each was constructed from prefabricated modules.

About 200 Liberty ships were lost due to enemy action in World War II. Their slow speed of 11 knots made them easy to attack by air, by sea, and by submarine, and often put them and their entire convoy at greater risk from submarine attack and from enemy surface vessels.

Fig. 23. Liberty ship SS *Zebulon Pike*. The record for building one of these ships was four days and eleven hours, but it usually took from one to two months. The hull was 441 feet 6 inches long and 56 feet wide, with a draft of 27 feet, 8-7/8 inches. The engine was a three-cylinder, triple expansion, reciprocating steam engine and the horse power was 2,500 at 76 rm. Thirty-two tons of fuel were consumed per day, and it had a top speed of 11.5 knots. There were 52 crew members including a gun crew of 29 Navy personnel. Her five holds could carry 9,000 tons of cargo. (Source: *Give Me Liberty or Give Me Death.* See footnote 13.)

At the conclusion of World War II, when the desperate need for the Liberty ships was over, criticism of their construction appeared. Vice Admiral Emory Scott Land was Administrator of the War Shipping Administration and the U.S.. Maritime Commission was responsible for the creation and maintenance of a fleet of some 6,000 merchant ships. His outspoken response to some of the critics was "We did the best we could with the tools we had. We built the ships; the war was won; and if you don't like that you can go to hell."[13]

The "New" Victory Ship

The Victory ship, first launched in February, 1944, was similar to the Liberty ship, but slightly larger to carry more goods and supplies. Between 1944 and 1946, 534 Victory ships were built. They had modest defensive armaments, were manned by a Navy Armed Guard, and boasted a much more powerful engine than their predecessor. It was constructed with greater strength for long term Atlantic service. (See the photo of the SS *Bluefield Victory* on the book jacket.) Victory ships went on to play a leading role in the aftermath of the War, and carried aid to Europe during the era of the Marshall Plan. They also played a major role in the Korean and Vietnam wars.

---

[13] *Give Me Liberty or Give Me Death: The Story of the Liberty Ships of World War II and of the Zebulon Pike* (American Bureau of Shipping for the American Merchant Marine Museum, Sept. 2002), p.16.

As in the case of the Liberty ships, Victory ships also used production-line techniques in their construction. With a much more powerful engine, the speed of the Victory was 17 knots—a major improvement over the Liberty's 11 knots.

Voyages on the *Maritime Victory*

I made three round-trip voyages across the Atlantic from March 1946 to the end of August 1946. Our mission was to transport 1,500 German and Italian POWs to Europe and 1,500 American troops from Europe back to New York. The POWs actually wore black-and-white striped uniforms with big letters "P O W" on their backs. Up to that time, I had not realized there were prison camps in the United states during the war.

While carrying American troops back to the States, the Army-Navy rivalry showed up as soon as we hit some rough weather in the North Atlantic. Because there were always many soldiers who became seasick in rough weather, the sailors put garbage cans on deck to accommodate them better. A nasty trick was played on the soldiers because the cans were placed on the windward side instead of the leeward side! The soldiers also slept on cots arranged five high. This was no picnic in rough weather.

A Tense Moment

The most anxious time for me occurred at night during my 12 a.m. to 4 a.m. watch in the spring of 1946. We were entering the English Channel in a very thick fog. There was no navigation radar aboard, and the helmsman and I were alone on the bridge. The ship's speed was "slow ahead," and the sailor on the bow rang the ship's bell at frequent intervals. The ship's whistle was sounded every two minutes, as we slowly moved forward. The Channel in the spring of 1946 hadn't yet been cleared of floating mines.[14] My primary concern was not so much the floating mines, but more about the possibility that crucial navigational buoys might be missing or washed away, and not replaced since the end of the war.

---

[14] Dateline London: "Northwest European waters will not be cleared of mines to make them completely safe for shipping until the summer of 1947, the Admiralty announced today" (*The New York Times*, March 30, 1946).

Buoys were our sole means of navigation in this heavy fog. The presumed location of all buoys in the English Channel were readily published and located in our chart room. But recent issues of "Notice to Mariners" reiterated the warnings about errant buoys and drifting mines. As we made our way in the Channel, we were initially fortunate as the buoys seemed to be present as located on the chart. Then about half way along the Channel route, a buoy was missing. This was critical, as a change of course was indicated. Knowing the currents, our speed, and the ship's direction, there was no choice but to presume it was there, and make the indicated change in course. The bow of the ship continued to be virtually obliterated by heavy fog. It was a lonely and anxious time for me; minutes seemed like hours. You can't imagine the sense of relief when the subsequent buoy was on station! The rest of the journey went fine, the fog gradually burned off, and no mines were encountered. The ship, crew, and soldiers were unscratched, thank God! And we didn't "wind up on the rocks."

Over the past several decades, I realized that at the age of 19 I had enormous responsibility for the ship and all on board. Today all ships undoubtedly have radar or satellite direction-finders of some modern origin.

French Fishing Boats
French fishing boats could be a challenge in the English Channel, especially during daytime, as they seemed to delight in frequently crisscrossing our bow. Being smaller vessels, they had the right-of-way. This required frequent course changes to avoid a collision. Having experienced this scenario more than a couple of times, I became frustrated with this game and passed one fishing boat a bit more closely than usual. I can still see one of the French sailors standing on his deck gesturing as we passed. I don't recall any further mischief from the boats after this.

A View of Bremerhaven in 1946
While docked in Bremerhaven, I was impressed with the diligence of the German citizens working every day, and under lights at

Fig. 24. The SS *Maritime Victory* alongside a pier in Bremerhaven. (Source: U.S. Navy photo.)

night, seven days a week, 24 hours a day; they were busy repairing the streets and buildings, and cleaning up any residual rubble.

Relations with the Germans seemed cordial. Cigarettes were at a premium, and one of our crew bought a wonderful accordion, and another a Grundig radio, for not much more than a carton of cigarettes. The demand for cigarette butts picked off the street was keen, and these were often smoked again by being held by a toothpick if the butt was too short to be hand-held.

For the first time I saw large trucks pulling a second loaded truck—a common finding in the United States today, but seemed to be a rarity in the States 50 years ago.

A Sudden Roll of the Ship

When a sailboat heels over in a stiff wind, the occupants can actually be touching the water or at least get very wet. This happened to me while standing my 12 p.m. to 4 p.m. watch as Third Mate. I could see a squall forming on the horizon coming in our direction. As is the case in all ocean surface vessels, the bridge has a series of windows through which you can observe the ship's direction or another vessel that might be in the area, as well as obstructions in the ship's path. For example, in 1946, icebergs commonly broke loose and floated into the shipping lanes, especially during the month of April. While standing with my weight mainly on one foot and loosely holding on to the wooden railing below the windows, the ship suddenly took a major roll, throwing me off balance. I started flailing my arms, trying to grab a railing or something to hold on to, while heading straight for the open door and the sea a few feet away. (At sea, the wheelhouse door on the windward side is kept closed, but it is allowed to remain open on the leeward side as long as the weather and time of year allow.) Before going into the sea, I managed to grab the metal combing belonging to the open wooden door and held on until it rolled back in the other direction. That taught me to be less casual; the ocean has many unpredicatable tricks up its sleeve, such as rogue waves towering 90 feet or more.

Time to Start Princeton Pre-Med Program: Fall 1946

At the conclusion of the above voyages, and the beginning of college, I left my deck officer activities to begin my freshman year in

Fig. 25. Back to school: Blair Hall, Princeton University.

the fall of 1946 at Princeton University (Fig. 25). I had always hoped to be a physician, and the next four years were spent taking courses that would satisfy the pre-med requirements. I remained in the United States Naval Reserve (USNR) as a deck officer, and even completed a few Navy correspondence courses on the side. For a brief period, I traveled to Jersey City one night a week, where I taught basic navigation to enlisted Naval reservists aboard a de-commissioned destroyer escort. The college work load soon put an end to this.

Fig. 26. The ship depicted above, SS *Lane Victory*, was constructed in the same year and in the same shipyard (Los Angeles, CA) as the SS *Warwick Victory*. Both ships had the same specifications: Displacement: 10,750 tons; length 455 feet; beam 62 feet; draft 28 feet; speed 15.5 knots; one cross compound steam turbine producing 6,000 hp at 90 rpm. There are currently two preserved Victory ships frequently used for historic, day-long trips: The SS *American Victory* based in Tampa, Florida and the SS *Lane Victory* based in Long Beach, California. The tour aboard the SS *Lane Victory* includes mock enemy attacks by planes and use of guns on board (obviously not employing live ammunition). Upon the 50th anniversary of D-Day, the SS *Lane Victory*, with many of its original crew, sailed from California to Normandy Beach, France. (Source: U.S. Government photo.)

Chapter 6:

SS *Warwick Victory* (1947)

During the summer of 1947, between freshman and sophomore years at Princeton, I sailed once again as Third Mate aboard another Victory ship, the SS *Warwick Victory*. The ship transported bags of wheat to England, France, and Germany, under America's Marshall Plan (Fig. 27).

Fig. 27. Unloading wheat in Bremerhaven, West Germany.

One particular episode—another "small world" story—occurred during that summer and has remained in my memory for more than 55 years. While standing the 12 a.m. to 4 a.m. watch, at about one o'clock in the morning, and about half way across the Atlantic heading for Liverpool, England, I noted the running lights of a ship on the horizon. We were slowly overtaking it.

When two ships wish to communicate visually, but are quite a distance apart, they use two lights (each one sitting on top of the two forward kingposts holding the booms), instead of a standard blinker light on the bridge. Though the forward kingposts are mostly used for cargo handling, they can also serve as an additional blinker light for communication by allowing a broader target when transmitting over large distances. The other ship started sending "A...A"...(Morse code, Letter A, meaning, " I'm trying to communicate with you"), using the lights on his kingposts. I then answered that I would receive the message. The deck officer sent the message, "Who is the Third [Officer]?" I replied, "Haynes." He then replied, "Not William F. Haynes?" I replied, "Yes!" It turned out to be a Kings Point classmate, Paul Johnson. His ship was also bringing wheat to Europe as part of the Marshall Plan. We were both heading for Liverpool. We then agreed to meet at a certain highly recommended pub there. I was very excited about the chance connection occurring in the middle of the night, half way across the Atlantic, purely by blinking lights. I turned to the helmsman in a moment of great excitement and announced, with unrestrained glee, "The Third Mate on that ship was a classmate from the Academy!" He was totally unimpressed, and replied in a monotone voice, "Is that right!"

A more serious happening also etched in my memory was the sight of starving English children going through the garbage cans looking for food while we unloaded bags of wheat in Liverpool. This image confirmed the great need for food among so many people suffering from hunger among the post-war European nations.

A Busy Time at Medical School and Internship
By May 1950, I had graduated from Princeton and entered P&S. A great number of my Kings Point classmates, not already on active duty in the Navy, were called up for the Korean conflict in 1950. The Navy believed I would be more useful to them as a physician, and they would look forward to my presence following graduation from medical school and completion of a one-year internship.

Medical years were very busy and the years flew by. Memories of the sea were replaced by an ocean of medical textbooks and clinical work. Following my graduation from Columbia in 1954, I spent the next year as a medical intern at New York City's St. Luke's Medical Center. Interns were given free laundry service, a room in the hospital, free meals, and $65 a month. This was a busy time, and I learned a lot about practical medicine. We worked every weekday and every other night, and every other weekend. The weekend "off-call" started at noon Saturday, after medical rounds.

And so, after finishing medical school, and one year of medical internship, I was launched into a new career in the United States Navy, this time as a physician for a two-year active duty stint.

PART III

Ship's Medical Officer, United States Navy (1955 to 1957)

Fig. 28. USNS *General Harry Taylor*. Specifications: Displacement 9,950 tons
empty, 17,250 tons loaded; length 522 feet 10 inches; beam 71 feet 6 inches;
draft 26 feet 6 inches; speed 18 knots; complement 356; troop capacity, 3,224;
armament four single 5 inch/38 dual-purpose gun mounts, four twin 1.1 inch
gun mounts (replaced by four twin 40mm gun mounts), 15 twin 20mm gun
mounts; single steam turbine producing 8,500 hp driving a single shaft and
screw. (Source: U.S. Navy photo.)

Chapter 7:

USNS *General Harry Taylor* (T-AP–145): September 1955–November 1955

Active duty orders appeared, as promised, by July 1, 1955, upon my having completed the one-year internship. Along with a dozen other doctors, I reported to St. Alban's Naval Hospital on Long Island for a three-week-long orientation, including a review course in pediatrics. Each of us was now a newly-commissioned Navy physician, having the rank of Lt. jg. (MC), USNR. At the conclusion of the orientation, we were given our orders. I had dreams of being assigned to a ship such as an aircraft carrier or a destroyer—a "real" Navy ship—but instead wound up with—you guessed it—a troop ship once more. But this time, as the Ship's Medical Officer, I realized that the Navy desired doctors who had more than one year of internship in order to fill the billet for large vessels such as aircraft carriers or battleships.

The New Medical Officer

My first assignment with the brand new title of Ship's Medical Officer was to report to the USNS *General Harry Taylor*, tied up alongside a pier in the Brooklyn Navy Yard. I had never sailed as a deck officer on a ship with a C-4 hull (see Fig. 28). Several years had swiftly passed since I had been aboard any vessel at all and my four years away had been filled with medical school and an additional year as a medical intern. The *Taylor* also seemed a little worse for wear. Long gone were the remnants of its bright and cheery self so beautifully illustrated in earlier photographs.

My dreams of serving on a real Navy flagship by then had

vanished. I could only imagine John Wayne standing on the bridge of the *Taylor* in his dress whites, ready to set sail, as in the movie *The Sea Chase* (1955). To paraphrase a well-known adage: One can't judge the heart of a ship by its awesome appearance.

The crew turned out to be very professional and there was, in general, a good feeling amongst all on board. The armament had been stripped away and there was an assigned complement of Navy personnel consisting of a Lieutenant Commander, an Executive Officer, and handful of U.S. Navy petty officers. The Medical Department consisted of a Chief Hospital Corpsman, several nurses, and enlisted hospital corpsmen.

I was delighted to meet the Medical Officer, Dr. Steen, who would be making his final trip as a Naval Officer on the *Taylor*. The Navy evidently thought that it would be a good idea for the retiring doctor to remain on board for his last trip in order to share his experiences with the replacement physician. We would walk around the sick bay, and he would explain his ideas about its management. He discussed with me the importance of the daily medical log book and answered my questions about the procedures regarding the dispensary. He pointed out the x-ray machine, the orthopedic equipment, the location of the antibiotic cabinet, the full dental outfit, the location of the I-V sets and bottles of normal saline, the operating and examining tables, and the two double-decker beds, among other things.

Soon after arriving, I assumed additional duties as Ship's Medical Officer, which included inspecting the ship's galley daily and examining closely the food preparation equipment. In addition, refrigerated food items left at room temperature for more than five hours were to be discarded. It was imperative that shipborne infections be avoided.

It was not long before the *Taylor* was on its way to Germany, the mission being to transport 1,500 United States troops for deployment in Europe. Then we were to return another 1,500 troops to New York City, where they were slated for discharge from military service.

The first trip was quite uneventful, but it did serve as a preview of trips to come, which included how to treat the ubiquitous series of seasick passengers as well as those with other medical problems, none of them life-threatening. At the conclusion of his last voyage, Dr. Steen then packed up his gear and readied himself for his own Navy discharge. I thanked him for his help, and wished him good luck. I believe he was returning for a residency in pathology.

This voyage was followed by several more, again transporting 1,500 troops both ways between Bremerhaven and New York. The *Taylor* eventually required time in dry dock for routine maintenance, repairs, and safety checks. All active duty personnel on board then left the ship and waited for our next assignment.

Fig. 29. USS *General George M. Randall*. The ship was built in the Federal Ship Building & Dry Dock Company, Kearny, NJ, and launched on June 30, 1944. She was assigned to MSTS in October 1949 and eventually transferred to the National Defense Reserve Fleet, James River, Fort Eustis, Va. Her length was 622 feet 7 inches, her beam was 75 feet 6 inches; and her draft was 25 feet 6 inches. Her speed was a fast 20.6 knots and she had twin propeller shafts, steam turbines, and 17,000 h.p. The hull design type was P2-S2-R2, with twin stacks. Troop capacity was 5,142, and the ship's crew numbered 465. (Source: U.S. Navy photo.)

Chapter 8:

USS *General George M. Randall* (AP–115): November 1955, three weeks

The Commandant at MSTS in New York assigned me to Temporary Assigned Duty (TAD) for a three-week trip as Ship's Medical Officer on the USS *General George M. Randall* (AP-115). The mission was the same as on the *Taylor*, that is to say, transporting around 1,500 troops and dependents both ways across the Atlantic, between New York and Bremerhaven.

The *Randall* trip was a short and pleasant diversion for me as Ship's Medical Officer. It was nice being on board an all Navy vessel. The *Randall* was well maintained, with better facilities and a longer turn-around time in port. The dispensary and its equipment were up-to-date, and the medical hospital corps and nurses were very capable. We also had two chief Hospital Corpsmen as part of the departments. (Besides its original mission of transport, the ship, sadly, had been the first to bring Korean War dead back to the United States in March 1951.)

Pl. 12

No medical emergencies occurred during the trip, aside from the usual 50 to 100 passengers a day being treated for seasickness, depending on the condition of the sea. But one day following a spell of rough seas, it dawned on me that I was fast becoming an "expert" on treating this illness—for whatever that's worth.

Seasickness and Tetany

It may seem at first glance, that while plowing through the North Atlantic in rough weather, we could have up to 100 dispensary

Fig. 30. Bow of the USS *General George M. Randall*. At the top of the picture, the *Randall* is flying the American "Union Jack" flag from the jackstaff, with 48 white stars on a blue background, as is customarily done on moored U.S. Naval vessels between 8:00 a.m. and sunset. Also note the sailor standing on the anchor hanging from the port side of the ship. There is a rat guard fastened to the hawser on the starboard side. (Source: U.S. Navy photo.)

visits on a given day related to problems concerning seasickness. This being the case, a few words on this subject, as well as the related subject of tetany, are in order.

Seasickness has been around for thousands of years. Nausea is always present, and can be the earliest sign. This widespread complication is derived from *naus*, a Greek word for nausea and refers to the English word for ship. It should therefore be of no surprise to discover that "seasickness" goes back to antiquity, an entity combining nausea with a ship's motions.

Motion sickness can also be associated with other conditions such as air and train travel, roller coasters, and from visual stimulation as in certain videos—just to name a few origins. The condition is generally accepted to be due to a mismatch of vestibular (inner ear) and visual sensations.

While traveling west under the Golden Gate Bridge aboard the *Cape Catoche* at the time of my first voyage, an unsettled stomach was the earliest symptom of seasickness, which fortunately passed away after about 20 minutes. For those not so fortunate, the symptoms may become prolonged and more pronounced: Sweating and vomiting, followed by dehydration, hyperventilation, and acute anxiety. In the worse case scenario, the patient could develop tetany leading to loss of consciousness.

Tetany, therefore, can be the end result of a prolonged bout of seasickness. The nerves within the body become irritable and send impulses to the muscles, which in turn undergo spasms resulting in cramped and bunched fingers, flexed wrists, severe spasms in the feet and legs, tremors, and possible loss of consciousness. Spasm of the larynx (laryngospasm) may lead to airway obstruction and possible asphyxiation, but I know of no one who died from this.

As I shall explain in the next chapter, those of us on the medical staff noticed that the percentage of passengers with seasickness on the *General Langfitt* seemed to be greater than among American troops and dependents seen on former ships. We became convinced that seasickness was not only due to motion aberrations, but a number of other factors could be contributing to this condition (see pages 84-85).

Fig. 31. USNS *General W.C. Langfitt*. The *Langfitt* was a C-4 type transport that was also part of the fleet of ships under the aegis of the MSTS. The ship was launched July 17, 1944, by the Kaiser Ship Yard, Richmond, California, and was commissioned by the Navy in September 1944 as an attack transport. Interestingly, one of the ship's early missions consisted of carrying marines from San Diego to Pearl Harbor for a brief stop, and then on to Eniwetok and finally to Saipan. Coincidently, this was the same route that the SS *Cape Catoche* had taken when I was a cadet midshipman, though we made the trip a month earlier, in August 1944. Similar to the *Taylor*, the *Langfitt* displaced 9,950 tons, was 522 feet long, and 71 feet, 6 inches wide, and had a draft of 24 feet. The average speed was 16 knots. During the height of World War II, its crew was composed of 356 officers and men, and she could transport 3,343 troops. This ship in World War II was well armed: Carrying four 5-inch cannons and sixteen 20mm machine guns, it was more like a small battleship than just a troopship. She was decommissioned in June 1946 only to be reacquired by the Navy in March 1950. During the Hungarian Revolution, the *Langfitt*, along with another C-4, USNS *General Harry Taylor*, were among the primary vessels carrying new immigrants to the States at that time. (Source: U.S. Navy photo.)

Chapter 9:

USNS *General W.C. Langfitt* (AP–151): November 1955–August 1956

Upon ending my TAD of 21 days with the USS *General George M. Randall*, I was next assigned to the USNS *General W.C. Langfitt* in November 1955. This was certainly not a sought-after assignment. Like the *Taylor*, the *Langfitt* was also an aging boxer Pl. 13 that had seen better days. Having participated in many wartime trips, she was no longer a new and shiny spring chicken. Her armament by this time had also been removed.

The *Langfitt*'s New Role: Transporting Immigrants

The Commandant in charge of MSTS in the Brooklyn Navy Yard ordered all physicians under his command to make a minimum of three round trips transporting immigrants before requesting a transfer, knowing that this was an exhausting but necessary assignment. There was a small Navy contingent on board, and the turn-around time, as it turned out, was brief: We had only two or three days layover on each side of the Atlantic. A crossing could easily take from seven to ten days depending on the season and the variable weather conditions.

This was the time of the unsuccessful Hungarian Revolution (1955–56).[15] Individuals who had escaped from "Iron Curtain"

---

[15] Some background to this revolution may be useful: After Germany's defeat in World War II, Joseph Stalin made Hungary a Communist satellite and placed Matyas Rakosi in charge. Following Stalin's death, Rakosi was replaced by Imre Nagy who started a program of reforms. However, he became too liberal in Soviet eyes. In April 1955, Rakosi was brought back by the Russian leaders, which resulted in Nagy's loss of political power. In February 1956, Nikita Khrushchev deposed Rakosi, replacing him with a strong-armed pro-Soviet leader, Erno

Fig. 32. Dr. Bruno Schultz aboard the *Langfitt*.

countries were to be our passengers. They had gathered in special locations in West Germany while awaiting sponsorship by American religious or secular agencies. Some had purposely changed their names while waiting for the trip to America. This was to protect family members who remained in Europe. (See also "Conversations on Deck," pages 89–90, for a further explanation.)

The USNS *General Langfitt*, unlike many of the other ships administered by MSTS, was a U.S. Navy ship, but it was unique in

Gero, who became prime minister in October 1956. By late October, students demanded that Nagy be reinstalled and Soviet troops withdrawn. Gero, as Prime Minister, rejected the students' demands and ordered the Hungarian soldiers to control crowds of demonstrators. Thousands were killed and wounded. The public, now very angry, banded together to fight Gero's regime. Ultimately, Soviet troops were called in to put down the progressively unruly demonstrations against the existing regime. In a conciliatory move, Nagy replaced Gero as Prime Minister, while Janos Kadar became chief of the Communist Party. Nagy desired to open up Parliament to other parties, and requested removal of the Soviet troops stationed in Hungary and the withdrawal of Hungary from the Warsaw Pact. On October 30, 1956, Soviet troops began to withdraw from Hungary, but Khrushchev, fearing loss of control, ordered Soviet troops to re-enter Hungary, and on November 4 began a 10-day campaign to regain total control of the country. Nagy fled to the Yugoslavian Embassy and, having been promised safe passage by Kadar, left the embassy but was captured, imprisoned, put on trial, and executed. In 1958, Kadar reinstituted Communist reign within Hungary and ruled as the Communist leader from 1956 to 1988. As many as 200,000 refugees escaped from Hungary to other countries in Europe and abroad. Of these, 40,000 made their way, largely via U.S. transport ship, to the United States.

that it was under a temporary contract with the Intergovernmental Committee for European Migration (ICEM), with headquarters in Geneva, Switzerland.[16]   Pl. 14

For purposes of communication, the common language spoken on board was German when dealing with passenger issues. Orders that concerned the passengers were transmitted over the ship's loudspeaker and would be heard by all of us on board. An example would be the call for dinner: *Achtung! Achtung! Alle passagierin: Das Essen ist serviert.* It was a strange feeling to be aboard a U.S. Naval vessel and hear messages being broadcast "auf Deutsch." Though I had taken one summer semester of German at Columbia before entering medical school, I was far from fluent in the language. The headquarters in Geneva, sensing that there might be problems with language, fortunately sent a German doctor, Bruno Schultz, to help as an interpreter (Fig. 32). He turned out to be a very pleasant older man with a gentle disposition, and reminded me of someone who could very well have been a violinist in the Hamburg Symphony Orchestra. Although he had been drafted into the German army during World War II, this mild mannered man in his fifties was a most unlikely prototype for a German military officer. Within days, we had developed a close friendship, and I would often visit his home and family in Bremen during the very short times we were in the German port. He, likewise, spent time at my home in Orange, New Jersey. Both his wife and small son were splendid people, and I accepted his offer to be Godfather to his son. We kept in touch for the next 15 years until time, distance, and attrition took its toll.

Over time, listening to all the announcements on the ship's loudspeakers became a burden as well. (The bonus for me was that I came to be a bit more fluent in the language as time went on.)

One of my functions as Ship's Medical Officer was to be stationed by the gangway each time the ship boarded a new group of refugees, making sure none of those beginning the ten-day voyage

---

[16] The International Refugee Organization (IRO), a temporary agency of the United Nations, was established in 1946 to arrange for the care and the repatriation or resettlement of Europeans made homeless by World War II. In 1952, the Agency was superseded by the Office of the United Nations High Commissioner for Refugees (UNHCR). UNHCR was awarded the Nobel Peace Prize in 1954.

Fig. 33. Youngsters aboard the *Langfitt*.

was suffering from any obvious physical handicap or appeared to be clinically ill.

You could easily sense the mixture of joy and sadness among many of these new immigrants. With each new group, I could sense an excitement mixed with some uneasiness. I noticed their joy of going to America, but I could also sense a degree of sadness in leaving their homeland, family, friends, and culture behind.

For most of the passengers, the only clothes they owned were those they were wearing. The children were precious: scrubbed faces, a cap, lederhosen, white socks, and often clasping a stuffed animal (Fig. 33). Each child could be identified by a tag hanging on a chain around his or her neck, listing name, sponsoring agency in the States, and a passenger identification number.

Pl. 15

Though many obstacles and dangers had been overcome in the process of escaping, they now had to face a different set of unknown challenges. One of these soon became apparent shortly after arriving on board: Everyone went through the required lifeboat drill, and passengers were assigned to specific life boats.

Pl. 16

The ship was also unusual in another way. We carried a handful of young German nationals, former graduate students from a number of excellent American universities, whose role was to give lectures to the passengers about "Life in America" while the ship made its way across the Atlantic. The dubious pay off for them was to be able to enjoy a couple of days in New York before the ship once again returned to Germany. I believed that these German nationals were to be the likely leaders of post-war Germany. Due to their fluent English, we all enjoyed many interesting conversations about the war and Germany's post-war future. The trip back to Germany was less hectic due to the fact that we carried fewer passengers when traveling in that direction. At these times, besides the crew, various officials from the United States often joined us. There were also five or six administrators who represented ICEM and who were responsible for the administrative paperwork and other details required of all immigrants coming to the United States.

We had a well-equipped dispensary (Fig. 34), including dental, orthopedic, and surgical tools as well as an operating table and an adequate supply of medications and intravenous medications, four hospital beds, and a treatment table. There was also a mobile

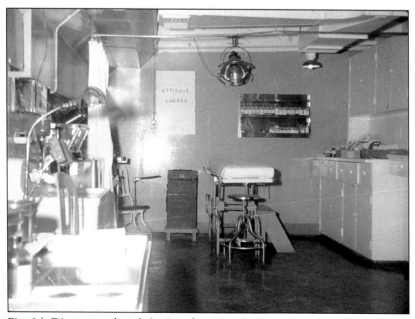

Fig. 34. Dispensary aboard the *Langfitt*. (Not shown are two double deck hospital beds.)

x-ray machine available. The medical staff included four nurses, eight hospital corpsmen, a Chief hospital corpsman, and yours truly, the Naval physician. The C.O. carried the rank of Lt. Commander. In addition, a Chaplain and a young Executive Officer were part of the Navy complement. The rest of the crew was composed of American civilians.

Between trips, while in New York, I remember making a couple of quick visits to my surgical friends at St. Luke's Medical Center for a refresher course (mainly to build my confidence) in handling acute surgical conditions that might arise, such as a hot appendix. The consensus regarding the latter seemed to be to put a drain in the abdomen, bed rest, and rely on intravenous fluids and antibiotics until a shore hospital could be reached. Naïvely or not, I nevertheless felt confident that I could handle almost any medical condition.

As I look back, while serving on the *Langfitt*, we transported 2,500 men, women, and children with each voyage. By the end of 12 such voyages, a total of 30,000 passengers successfully completed the trip to America. I was grateful that during those trips no one died at sea, and there was no reason for any major surgery.

It was an exciting time for me for a number of reasons. Many of the adult escapees would share their unique stories dealing with their flight to freedom. As mentioned, I fortunately kept a diary noting many of these tales, some of which follow.

Adventures in Dentistry

An oral surgeon joined us for one voyage as part of his yearly two weeks of Navy Reserve duty. He added a new dimension to my job by instructing me in the use of some of the dental tools he found in our dispensary. A great majority of these passengers showed evidence of very poor dental health. Under the watchful eye of our one-trip oral surgeon, I started doing some dental work when there was a lull in medical care. By the time my nine months aboard the *Langfitt* ended, I had performed over two-dozen dental extractions—mainly due to abscesses, while others were due to retained roots. Flushed with apparent success, I dared to expand my horizons by fixing a few dental plates and filling a few cavities. The patients were grateful, and I found it to be a fulfilling sideline for an "amateur"; fortunately, there were no complications.

A Small World Story

Another story that I remember clearly was an evening where four or five of us were sitting around a table in the officers' lounge, chatting while enjoying a cup of coffee. We were traveling back to Bremerhaven with only the usual handful of officials as passengers. A new German doctor, Heinz, had replaced Bruno for one trip. He had a "Prussian" type of personality, the opposite of my older German colleague. Our ship's Third Engineer officer joined the conversation as talk evolved around World War II. He mentioned that during the war his parents remained in Germany and he served in the U.S. Merchant Marine. Furthermore, his previous ship had been torpedoed and sunk during the Murmansk run. (This particular shuttle was very dangerous, and contained a large area of the Atlantic called "submarine alley." Convoys traveling along this stretch of water about half way between North America and Murmansk were often on their own with insufficient ship or air cover [Fig 35]. The speed of the convoy was adjusted to the slower speed of the Liberty ships, and Nazi subs would line up and knock off [torpedo] the ships like sitting ducks.) Heinz, the new German

Fig. 35. Atlantic convoy underway. (Source: U.S. Department of Transportation, Maritime Administration, Washington, DC.)

doctor, asked the Third Engineer very detailed questions such as: the name and description of his ship, the year, month and day it was attacked, and the location of the sinking. The engineer replied, in turn, to each of the questions posed by the doctor. There was a brief pause, followed by a deafening silence when the doctor replied, "I was the U-boat commander that sank your ship." A small world story!

When the war ended, Heinz had gone on to medical school, but still retained a more "military" than "medical" persona even after all those years.

Seasickness and Tetany: The Emotional Factor and Therapy

While aboard the *Langfitt*, the majority of illnesses were due to seasickness, and we logged about 100 cases a day for this malady. Others were brought down to us with tetany; that is to say, severe muscle spasms of the upper extremities and hands due to excess vomiting, dehydration, and hyperventilation.

The emotional parameter was certainly greater among these escapees. Many had lost homes, their culture, friends and families. They were not fluent in English (the language of their new country), and likewise the various members of the crew were not versed in German. Where was the "anchor," the authority figure, someone who understood the ways of the sea and with whom they could vent their feelings? In a very limited way I attempted to reassure those who were brought to the dispensary and whose condition warranted a brief stay, but reassurance had its limits. True enough, yet I couldn't help but notice a sense of peace among those passengers who, when resting in the dispensary, had been almost hysterical when admitted. After I consulted with them, they seemed to have found some semblance of an anchor.

In the same vein, the majority of the *Langfitt* passengers had never voyaged for seven to ten days across a large ocean and did not know what to expect. I recall a patient who was worried that if the ship sank, she would likely drown. The smells, the crowded conditions, stressful memories from their flight from Iron Curtain countries only compounded their fears. Dehydration and lack of adequate food intake all played a role in a sense of helplessness. A panic attack might ensue, complete with rapid shallow breathing (hyperventilation) and a subjective sense of "not enough air." The result of this could, in many cases, lead to respiratory alkalosis whereby the blood CO_2 falls, the bicarbonate and pH rise, and simultaneously, the ionized calcium in the blood stream falls. Early symptoms of tetany would be manifested by tingling of fingers, toes, and around the mouth. The treatment for tetany in these more advanced cases and in my experience responded to intravenous fluids and intravenous calcium, and rest for a few hours in the dispensary supplemented by a large dose of reassurance. I found it worthwhile to try a few alternative treatments to halt the progression to early symptoms of seasickness. These included staying on deck facing the wind and remaining amidships, rather than being on the forward or aft parts of the ship because the latter two locations accentuate the ship's up and down motions. Saltines and an apple while on deck seemed to help as well. Other hints were: to avoid odors in the compartments during the day, to look at the horizon when on deck, and to not lie flat. Needless to say, at times "nothing works."

Never Question the "Oberartz" (Doctor)

I remember one poor "frau" who was brought down to sick bay carried by four male passengers, each man grasping one of her four extremities. Frightened, she felt she was going to die from the vomiting and dehydration. These observations were compounded by her concern that she couldn't swim! I learned very early in my orientation that the German mind set was "never question the Oberartz." Whatever the doctor said was always correct, and by obeying all instructions, there surely would be a good outcome. In order to fit into this pattern on board the *Langfitt*, I had to adopt a slightly different attitude from that learned in my internship. When dealing with this cultural background divergence, for example, the simple act of closing the curtain in the dispensary had to be accomplished with great flare! Once more, there would be little room for questions. We kept a bottle of sterile water in the dispensary, labeled *Medizin gegen Seekrankheit*. This woman illustrated the point. The curtain having been dramatically closed, the nurse had the "gnädige frau" bend over the treatment table and pulled down her panties. I very purposefully drew up in a syringe about 2cc's of the "powerful medicine" and slapped the solution into her buttocks. She jumped up, walked back to her cabin area, and was immediately "cured." No questions asked!

On one occasion, another frau arrived at our dispensary obviously seasick, and quite hysterical. Trying to comfort her I wanted to say: "No one dies from seasickness." But using my limited German, I said, *Neun Mann stirbt von Seekrankheit*, which she (almost correctly) interpreted as "nine men are dying from seasickness." Upon hearing this, she slowly sank to the deck. The words of comfort I meant to say were: *Niemand stirbt von Seekrankheit*, which means "No one dies from seasickness." Despite my bad German, she recovered.

Seasickness: Antidote or Anecdote?

Despite all the scientific advances in medicine over the past century, sometimes there is nothing the passenger can do to either avoid or treat the *mal de mer*. In fact, more than once I've witnessed passengers coming on board, especially Army dependents, complaining of dizziness while the ship was still tied up at the pier. Their problem was: They started taking Dramamine at home a few days before boarding the ship and were suffering a side effect from the medicine.

One day a distraught and exhausted, but peeved, middle-aged woman arrived in the dispensary for the fifth time in five days: *Für fünf Tage habe ich gar nicht gegessen* ("I have not eaten anything for five days!"). She then recited all the remedies we had suggested: Dramamine tablets, injections, apples and saltines, one quart of Pepsi Cola, rectal Dramamine, and even resting on deck in the fresh air for most of every day. She said, *"Ich habe aufgegeben. Alles ist kaputt!"* (literally, "I have surrendered. Everything is broken," which, interpreted, would mean "I give up. It's all over for me.") Bless her heart. Fortunately for all of us, we were approaching New York, and she survived.

Any Port in a Storm

There was only limited space for luggage due to the cramped quarters (Fig. 36); the sleeping compartments consisted of bunks that were overcrowded and often stacked five high. The women were located in cramped quarters, while women with young children had

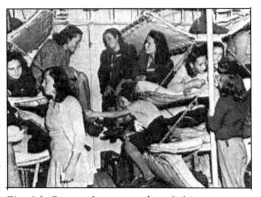

Fig. 36. Cramped quarters aboard ship.
(Source: http://www.usmm.org/dp.html)

small cabins, and the men were located in separate compartments.

An elderly lady came to the dispensary looking for another cabin. She could not sleep, she said, since there were two children, three women, and a crib all crowded together. The small space and noise were overwhelming her. Unfortunately, she was told that all the cabins were occupied, and she was quite unhappy with this report. We did not see her for two days, and a nurse and I decided to visit her cabin to see how she was coping. We found her—sleeping peacefully curled up in the crib.

Locked Out

It was 2 a.m. in a chilly February on one of our many voyages across the Atlantic. The Navy C.O. had his sleep disturbed by an unlatched watertight door that was banging against the bulkhead outside his cabin with every roll of the ship. Dressed only in his skivvies, he opened his cabin door and hooked the banging steel door. Suddenly he realized he had locked himself out. The night watchman came by and noted the C.O., with skivvies waving in the breeze, trying to figure how to get back into his room. (The porthole was obviously too small to crawl through.) Fortunately, the watchman saw his predicament, returned with special keys, and reopened the cabin door. The Commander ordered the watchman not to mention this episode to anyone. At the Commander's re- Pl. 17 quest, of course, this episode was kept quiet.

An Amorous Encounter

A full moon, calm seas, mid-July, and a dance on deck had all the potential for a Hollywood movie. The scene suddenly changed when an overly amorous fräulein passenger cornered a fellow male passenger, lost her footing, and slid down a stairwell cutting her lip. The cut responded to an antiseptic and a bandage. The nurse, while smiling, suggested that cold sitz baths twice daily for 15 minutes might help control her amorous ways.

An Ear Infection ("Ohrenschmerzen")

A 12-year-old Polish girl appeared in our dispensary complaining of a pain in her ear due to an inner ear infection. I gave her liquid antibiotic along with the instruction that it was medicine for her earache and to take two teaspoons four times a day and return if not better. She returned in two days and claimed the ear was no better. She then cupped her hand to her ear and gestured saying, "I can only get one teaspoon four times a day into the ear." We often fail to appreciate certain assumptions when we prescribe medications for people of different cultures!

Precision in Following Directions

There is another difference, perhaps unique, with our German patients' culture and ours when it comes to following medication directions. Not all our passengers were complaining of seasickness. As mentioned above, some had a variety of other diagnoses requiring antibiotics. In those instances, I would say, for example, *Eine tablette vier mal am Tag, mit Wasser* ("Take one tablet four times a day with some water"). The individual would then look at his or her watch, which might be 3:56 p.m., and you could bet your bottom dollar at precisely four hours later, at 7:56 p.m., he or she would take the next dose. Often there would be a subsequent question: "Should I take the tablet with a quarter glass, a half glass, or a whole glass of water?" How precise! These little hints later came in handy when I ultimately began private practice of medicine.

Swinging Steel Doors and Finger Tips

There were a number of finger tips that were lost when an individual grabbed the metal combing of a swinging unhooked steel door. The door would open with the ship's roll, and then slam shut when the ship rolled back in the other direction, sometimes catching the fingers in the process. One time a man brought me a remnant of his finger tip, and I was able to sew it back on. It seemed to be healing when we docked several days later, but only time would tell.

Conversations on Deck

One day while the ship was underway for New York, I had a conversation with a middle-aged Polish gentleman on deck. He mentioned that he and another Polish friend had purposely changed their names to protect the remaining family members in Poland, a practice I have already mentioned. Evidently his friend had taken an earlier voyage and was now living in an apartment in Chicago. In the course of our conversation, the passenger remarked, "My friend, now living in Chicago, wrote to tell me that he had received a post card sent to his new address but using his former Polish name." It was sent by the Polish secret police, as much as saying, "We know where you are." This was a cause of great concern as he worried about retributions against his family.

Another passenger, a Czech about 45 years old, was a former worker in the Skoda munitions plant and had joined other workers in a strike against the Russian forces there. He said to me, "Do you know how the Russians stopped the strike? They would randomly knock on the doors of those living in the area and pull out the men. We never knew which door the authorities would choose next. Those chosen were taken to a nearby field. One hundred men were shot for every day of the strike. The strike didn't last very long!"

I once found myself in conversation on deck with a former farmer from Hungary, 65 years of age, whose ultimate destination was the state of Washington. He exclaimed with great enthusiasm, "I just can't wait to begin farming again!" It struck me that he was of the age when working people in the States were dreaming of retiring.

Having learned that a Yugoslavian physician was a passenger on board, I located him and started a conversation. He was about

50 years old, and I asked where in the States he would be living. He replied he would be living in the outskirts of Detroit, and he was being sponsored by a former American pilot. During the war the American's plane was hit by ground fire, forcing him to bail out and land in a field near the doctor's home. The physician rescued the pilot and arranged for his safe return to the Allied lines. The former pilot never forgot this act of courage on his behalf. He was now sponsoring the doctor to come to America, and had even arranged for interviews for him at the local hospital.

Don't Wave Those Blood-shot Eyes at Me!

The Master-at-Arms (M.A.) of the USNS *General Langfitt* was awakened one morning by someone incessantly knocking on his cabin door following a long night of merriment when the ship was docked in Bremerhaven. He woke up and staggered to the door to find a German man with a large package for him, saying that he wanted $10.00. The M.A. did not remember buying this parcel, but because he saw his signature on the outside, and desiring to obtain more rest, he gave the man the $10.00. Two hours later, he arose, dressed himself, and opened the package. Within the large bundle were three small toy monkeys, with red eyes worth not more than 40 cents, connected by a long elastic band! Fortunately, the time in port was short, and the great majority of the crew had enough time to relax and stay out of any serious trouble.

Pl. 18

"A Team Effort"

A frightened woman passenger ran to our ship's dispensary stating that a lady in one of the forward compartments was very sick, unable to move, and having severe cramps in her hands and feet. Believing that this was another case of tetany, I told the woman to get assistance from some of the male passengers and bring the lady to the hospital dispensary. After several minutes, the ship's loudspeaker blared out, "Dr. Haynes, please report immediately to the forward compartment!" Upon arrival at said location, I could see that the lady was indeed having a severe bout of tetany, but was not really critically or seriously ill. I found her, however, lying

Fig. 37. Children at Christmas party aboard ship docked at Bremerhaven.

prostrate on a couch, her fingers held in the characteristic cramped position, moaning, and her eyes half-closed. Pandemonium was breaking out everywhere: Children were crying and fellow women passengers were greatly upset. A man was perched on top of the patient, pumping her arms in the air in an attempt to give artificial respiration, and the Navy C.O. was there trying to maintain order. Mr Regamey (the ICEM Escort Officer) was shouting in the distressed woman's ear, and asking for her husband's name and her ship's ID number! We brought her to the dispensary. Despite rumors that she died from a heart attack, the patient did well following intravenous calcium gluconate, fluids, and bed rest for a few hours.

St. Nicholas is Coming to Town

At Christmas time, I was St. Nicholas on board ship for a large number of children, many of whom were orphans. Though the pillow kept slipping from the front of my Santa's outfit, no one Pl. 19 seemed to complain, and the children enjoyed the celebration immensely (Fig. 37).

Fig. 38. Displaced persons aboard ship view the Statue of Liberty.
(Source: http://www.usmm.org/dp.html)

The Statue of Liberty

There were too many human interest stories to list them all, but the greatest story for me was witnessing the loud cheers mixed with tears of gratitude as we passed the Statue of Liberty when the *Langfitt* finally entered New York harbor. It seemed that the ship listed to the port side when every man, woman, and child crowded the ship's railing (Fig. 38) to view this symbol of our great country, a hallmark of freedom and opportunity. The overwhelming appreciation exhibited by these new arrivals never ceased to touch me, and the magic moment never lost its appeal even after 12 voyages. It also reminded me that all people, regardless of background, deserve a chance to work, raise a family, and hope for a life of happiness. Now, before their very own eyes stood that emblem of hope and opportunity.

Sea Time Aboard the USNS *General W.C. Langfitt*

Reminiscing about the USNS *General Langfitt* experience, I realized that it was all worthwhile and that I had a small part to play as history was being made. During my stint from December 1955 to August 1956, no serious emergencies (thankfully) had occurred. I hoped that I had made a small difference in many of the new immigrants' lives; they certainly had left an unforgettable impact upon me.

So much for a series of sea stories that I fortunately preserved in a daily sea log over those years; they serve as a chronicle for human perseverance, humor, and achievement—and even Man's inhumanity to Man in time of War. Now, 50 years later, it seems an appropriate time to share some of these tales. They belong to our nation's story as well. It was a time when America was the model for moral leadership. My hope is that the great majority of these former passengers have been happy and successful over the years since their arrival in the States. For me, dealing with individuals from many nations and from all walks of life was a first-hand education.

Fig. 39. USNS *Pvt. Elden H. Johnson.* Keel laid down, June 3, 1941, as Alcoa Corsair, a Maritime Commission type (C-2) hull, under Maritime Commission contract (MC hull 176), at Moore Dry Dock Co., Oakland, CA. Launched on December 4, 1941, she was acquired by the Navy and Commissioned USS *Pinkney* (APH-2), November 27, 1942. Decommissioned on September 9, 1946, she was transferred to the Maritime Commission and simultaneously to the U.S. Army Transportation Service and converted to a Transport at Puget Sound Shipbuilding and Dry Dock Co. Commissioned by the US Army Transportation Service as USAT *Private Elden H. Johnson*, she was transferred to the Navy on March 1, 1950, and assigned to the Military Sea Transportation Service (MSTS) and placed in service as USNS *Pvt. Elden H Johnson* (T-AP-184). Placed out of service on December 27, 1957, she was transferred to the National Defense Reserve Fleet, Hudson River, N.Y. The C-2 types were designed by the United States Maritime Commission in 1937–38. They were all-purpose cargo ships with five holds. Between 1940 and 1945, 173 such ships were built. The first C-2s were 459 feet long and 63 feet at the beam, with a maximum draft of 25 feet 7 inches and a speed of 15.5 knots. Later ships varied in size and speed. The *Pvt. Elden H. Johnson* had a speed of 18 knots. (Source: U.S. Navy photo.)

Chapter 10:

USNS *Pvt. Elden H. Johnson* (AP–184): August 1956–October 1956

The same Commandant in charge of MSTS based in Brooklyn Navy Yard raised the option of my going ashore for the remaining service time. I would be doing Navy physicals and recruiting work at a Navy recruiting center in Pittsburgh. It seemed boring to me at the time, and I requested that I be allowed to finish my service at sea. While awaiting permission from Bureau of Naval Personnel (BuPers) in Washington, I enjoyed temporary duty by being assigned two short trips to military bases in the Caribbean on the smaller MSTS ship, the USNS *Pvt. Elden H. Johnson*. This assignment turned out to be a gift: The trip was less hectic, and the calm waters of the Caribbean, the warm weather, and palm trees were a pleasant surprise. There were fewer troops and dependents, which added up to a more relaxed life for me as medical officer. We deployed troops and dependents and supplies in Cuba (Guantanamo Bay), Puerto Rico, and Panama. By the time I had finished two of these short trips, my request to stay at sea was approved by Washington. I retained the response from BuPers. Thinking I must be crazy to stay at sea, I could imagine the officer writing the letter and smiling as he noted in the last sentence of the paragraph: "We send you our best wishes for another seven months at sea." (No doubt the man preferred his active Navy duty on land—in Washington, D.C.)

Recollections
During our Caribbean ports of call, while alongside the pier and disembarking the dependants and troops, it came as a surprise to me to see a real Army band waiting for us. They played well— Pl. 20

95

some traditional John Philip Sousa's marches and even "Anchors Away!"—and it reminded me of a scene in the movies. For a fleeting moment, my mind turned to a Hollywood scene of a huge battleship or aircraft carrier with all hands on deck in their dress whites. I don't think I ever owned a dress white uniform because we wore sea-going khakis (Fig. 40), an exception being a Navy blue uniform in winter while ashore or on certain occasions for Sunday dinner at sea. Hearing the band playing, however, did give me a charge during the welcoming scene on the dock. The weather was delightful and the palm trees seemed to sway in time with the music—quite a change from the harsh conditions we saw in the North Atlantic.

The other recollection concerned the marine guards at gates to the military facilities. Their salutes were crisp and out of this world. Again there appeared a short flashback to a number of Hollywood films, but these were the real McCoy. I was proud of their military attitude and presence.

I had never before seen the Panama Canal, nor Panama City. The Pilot seemed very relaxed as we watched the ship being towed

Fig. 40. Dr. Bill Haynes at GTMO (Guantanamo Bay, Cuba) enjoying a freshly cut pineapple aboard the *Pvt. Elden H. Johnson*.

through the locks of the canal. For both trips, Panama City was our Pl. 21
last port of call. My Caribbean adventures were now ended. The
next port of call would be the Brooklyn Navy Yard.

Are You Right or Left-handed? Look at the Ear Drums
Awaiting my next ship assignment, I was placed on 10 days temporary duty helping out at the Brooklyn Navy Yard Dispensary.
During those few days, I encountered another Navy doctor—an
Ear, Nose, and Throat (ENT) specialist—who evidently had been
stationed there for many months. By this time, he was more than
ready to return to civilian life. What seemed to alleviate his frus-
trations while working in the dispensary was the fact that he had
gained the reputation for correctly predicting a patient's right- or
left-handedness by merely looking at an individual's ear drums. I
was fortunate to be present for his farewell party. The celebration
had a dual purpose: to wish him well and to find out the "secret of
the ear drums." The party was a success, complete with ice cream
and cake, and we now awaited the answer to the eardrum mystery!
His comments follow: Everyone who seeks medical attention first
fills out a brief form by answering each question with a check
mark, YES or NO.

Yes	No	
☑	☐	Have you had similar symptoms in the past?
☐	☐	Do you have any allergies?
☐	☐	Is it painful?
☐	☐	Are the symptoms confined to one ear?
☐	☐	Any fever or chills? Etc.

The doctor first quickly glanced at the checked boxes. When
a person is right-handed, the tail of the check mark points to the
patient's right shoulder and for those who are left-handed, the tail
of the checkmark points to the left shoulder. Then the doctor goes
through the ritual of examining the patient.

That was his secret! He then smiled, waved, thanked all present, and departed for civilian life!

Fig. 41. USNS *Geiger* at sea. This vessel, with a type designation of P2-S1-DN3, had a long and varied service with MSTS. Initially conceived as a vehicle carrier similar to the successful SeaTrain type vessels, they were converted into troop transports because of the urgent need to deploy troops overseas. At 532 feet in length, and 12,420 gross tons, they were some of the largest vessels built by the Maritime Commission during the Second World War. They could accommodate 228 officers, 3,595 men, and 6,840 tons of cargo, with a cruising speed of 17 knots. (Source: U.S. Navy photo.)

Chapter 11:

USNS *Geiger* (T-AP–197): October 1956–July 1957

Upon completion of two tours on the *Pvt. Eldon H. Johnson*, Bu-Pers had granted me permission to remain at sea. Orders arrived for me to be Ship's Medical officer on the USNS *Geiger*, one of the most modern troopships in the Navy at that time. It was now October, 1956.

The USNS *Geiger* was a beautiful vessel in all ways, especially in quality, quarters, and speed. The port layover time was longer, four to six days instead of the typical two to three days layover in the case of the *Langfitt*, and my role was again the same: Ship's Medical Officer. The mission had not changed in that we were to transport 1,500 American troops and dependents in both directions between New York and Bremerhaven.

Pl. 22

"Veterinarian" on Call

While underway to Germany, one of my first patients on the *Geiger* was a dog who had lost the end of his tail. Pets were kept on deck in screened boxes protected from the elements. Early on, we encountered some rough weather that must have jostled the dog's cage resulting in the sudden loss of the distal 25 percent of the pooch's tail. The owner brought the dog and the remnant of the tail to the dispensary. With the aid of lidocaine, bandage, and penicillin, the tail was reattached. I felt I had become not only an "amateur dentist," but now while on the *Geiger*, I could add "amateur veterinarian" to my Curriculum Vitae (C.V.). The dog's tail seemed to be in place four days later when we arrived in Bremerhaven, but don't ask if it was still in place two weeks later.

99

The Curse of "K.P."

Kitchen Police (K.P.) duty isn't always the most sought-after duty, especially aboard ship. There is always the hope among the troops that *someone else* might volunteer for the job. There was plenty of free time for the troops to take it easy either going to Europe in the mid-1950s as replacements or returning home. In either case, K.P. was one of the necessary daily chores to be carried out. There were other work details, but somehow dealing with garbage cans, cleaning dishes, peeling potatoes, and washing down the kitchen area was not high on a soldier's wish list. This meant that in order to capture enough kitchen help, the Bos'n or an Army sergeant, depending on the circumstances, had to be creative. Volunteers were scarce as hens' teeth. Yet it can be difficult to ascertain which troops hanging out in their compartments were "gold-bricking" and which were really seasick (Fig. 42). The chief Bos'n solved the problem by posting his men at each compartment exit, and then walking through a compartment spilling ammonia as he traveled. Those not really seasick immediately jumped up and ran for the exits where they were

Fig. 42. Seasick soldier.

captured by petty officers waiting for them and assigned to K.P. or other jobs.

The word somehow got out that a certain Army private on board was a Harvard Law School graduate. He chose the route of being drafted as a private for a two-year hitch rather than becoming an officer for a three-year stint. The poor soul was given the garbage disposal detail for most of the voyage to Europe. The reasoning behind this was not clear to me. Perhaps the M.A. had a thing about lawyers.

The Ups and Downs of a Navy Chaplain

The nuances and personalities present amidst folks living in a small town can also be found among those living aboard any ship. Most towns have a member of the clergy as well as pranksters and, not surprisingly, so did our ship, the *Geiger*. The Navy Chaplain's assistant was a very young, pleasant sailor who never drank, smoked, or used foul language. The *Geiger* had no sooner docked in Bremerhaven when a large group of sailors were given leave for several hours. A party was soon underway in a German beer parlor for one of the crew who was celebrating his last voyage before discharge. It was not long before our young "Jack Armstrong" (the All-American Boy and Chaplain's assistant), was "in the bag." He made it back to his bed on board the ship, but was evidently awakened three or four times by pounding on the cabin door. Each time he woke up, he found another sailor who was tipsy but evidently not tired enough to turn in. Finally, the pounding on the door occurred once too often. The young assistant lost control, and he called out in desperation, "Come in you S.O.B., etc., etc." (very vile language). Who should walk in but the pristine Chaplain himself! I wonder which of the two was more shocked!

On another occasion, the same Navy Chaplain, who was counting the minutes before he would be getting off the ship in New York, wanted to sell his suitcase, which was in need of a complete overhaul, for two dollars. A colorful enlisted man, named Kraft, thought he would go along with his offer and bought the tattered bag. Having done this, Kraft then proceeded to tell the Chaplain how he could fix it up, and in fact, he even knew someone who would pay five dollars for it. The Chaplain's expression perked up, and he appeared excited. He enquired if Kraft would sell it back for two dollars. Kraft laughed and replied that he would sell it back for three dollars and fifty cents. After much bickering, he sold it back to the Chaplain for three dollars, making a profit of one dollar. Kraft then walked out of the Chaplain's office with a big grin on his face. The story made the rounds of the ship that Kraft was only fooling; he really didn't know anyone who would pay five dollars for the bag. The sight of New York couldn't come soon enough for the Chaplain as this was his first, and hopefully for his sake, last trip on the *Geiger*.

The Navy Executive Officer called a meeting of the Military Department just before the *Geiger* was to leave for another trip to

Bremerhaven. He announced, "Men, I want you to meet the new Division Officer, Ensign West Boatsman." The young officer whispered to the Executive Officer, "The name is Wilcockson." The Executive Officer, obviously upset by his mispronouncing the name then replied, "Excuse me, Ensign West Coxswain." Realizing he mispronounced it wrong again, he said, "Oh well, coxswain, boatswain, it's all the same—they are all still a part of the Navy."

"Firewater" & Fireworks

The usual medical events that were common on the *Langfitt* were also seen while sailing on the *Geiger*; one could always count on lots of seasickness as well as other medical illnesses seen in any medical office. There was one unusual exception: The White Cliffs of Dover. These cliffs had a mysterious way of bewitching one or two soldiers every trip on the way home to the States. Almost like clockwork, I would be paged to report to the deck because a soldier was having a seizure! Symptoms could include tremors, hallucinations, and *grand mal* seizures.

Pl. 23

It takes about 36 hours for the *Geiger* to reach the White Cliffs after leaving Bremerhaven, and coincidentally, it takes about the same time for the symptoms of acute alcohol withdrawal to be manifested. Evidently, it was common practice for soldiers to do some serious drinking on the train traveling from Frankfurt to meet the ship in Bremerhaven, because once aboard ship, they knew they could not obtain any alcohol. Fortunately, with the help of infusions of vitamins, enough fluids, sedation, and bed rest, the alcohol effects abated, and all the folks with seizures recovered.

An Army corporal on the way back to the States was placed in our ship's hospital while recovering from alcohol-related auditory and visual hallucinations. Soon after admission, I asked him if he still thought he heard angels' voices. He replied, "At first I thought I must have been dreaming until I saw two angels standing in the corner of the room, then I knew it was no dream."

A career Air Force pilot, a captain with 20 years of service, was being sent back to the States for discharge due to "alcoholism." His job entailed flying aircraft for many hours across Europe. His food intake was limited during this time. By the time he returned to his base several hours later, he would be perspiring, and feeling shaky and confused. He always felt slightly better following a few shots of whiskey at the Officers' Club. His comrades, noting his condition after each flight, urged him to report to the base dispensary. The examining doctor noted the confusion, tremor, and unsteady gait along with the strong smell of alcohol on his breath. When this scene was repeated more than once, the doctors concluded that all of his symptoms added up to a diagnosis of alcoholism. It was recommended that he be discharged from the service. Adding to the captain's problems was the fact that his wife also believed he had become an alcoholic and was preparing to leave him. While traveling home on our ship, he had a seizure. A limited work-up revealed a low blood sugar, so we did frequent follow-up studies of blood sugar levels. It soon became apparent that he could be harboring an insulin-secreting tumor, an insulinoma (a pancreatic islet cell tumor causing insulin over-secretion). We managed to prevent his blood sugar from dropping by checking his blood glucose levels at regular intervals and giving him a high carbohydrate diet. (When a person's blood sugar drops too low, hypoglycemia occurs, and this can lead to seizure.) When we arrived in New York, he was transported to St. Alban's Naval Hospital in Long Island. I later found out that a happy ending ensued. The doctors agreed that his blood sugar had evidently dropped too low when on long flights in the Air Force, during which time his carbohydrate intake of food was minimal. This and further tests at the hospital confirmed an insulin secreting tumor. Following surgical removal of the tumor, the symptoms disappeared. His wife did not leave him, and he remained in the Air Force. The sugar in the alcohol "shots" following his long flights must have raised his blood sugar and temporarily made him feel better, but the symptoms were misinterpreted as due to alcoholism.

Greeting the Pilot

After being at sea, it is always exciting to see the Pilot boat drawing alongside of our ship . . . we soon would be ashore! The Pilot is licensed by his government and is totally familiar with the waterways, currents, winds, and navigational aids needed to guide the ship in entering as well as leaving the harbor. The Pilot and Pilot boat usually arrive quietly and unannounced. A rope ladder (referred to "Jacob's Ladder") is lowered down as the boat comes alongside. The Pilot merely climbs up the ladder, steps on to the main deck, and walks up to the ship's bridge where he takes charge of the vessel. With the ship's master alongside, the Pilot directs the course and speed of the vessel heading for or leaving its berth.

At one point, the *Geiger* was sent to Southampton, England, to pick up troops and dependents. Before entering the harbor, the word came over the intercom that this would be the last opportunity for all passengers to dump garbage over the fantail. (The fantail is the main deck of the ship nearest the stern.) One of the passengers, not knowing where the fantail of the ship was located, promptly grabbed two fully loaded scrap baskets from her cabin, ran to the side of the ship, and without looking below, emptied the entire contents over the side, just barely missing the head of the English Pilot who was at that moment climbing up the ladder to board the ship. The time for garbage dumping was changed to an hour before the expected arrival of the Pilot, and it was made known where the ship's fantail was located—thus avoiding any further misunderstanding.

Pl. 24

Fig. 43. Nameplate up high on the *Geiger*.

Higher Isn't Always Better

Being assigned to a cabin on one of the upper decks can be a mixed blessing aboard a troop transport like the *Geiger*, if the transatlantic crossing takes place during the winter season. Cabins on the higher decks experience a greater magnitude of roll in heavy seas. On the *Geiger*, generals, colonels, and other high ranking officials were typically assigned rooms topside. This arrangement seems fine when the ship is tied up dockside. I overheard a major's wife speaking to her spouse prior to sailing, "What a lovely room, George, and up so high!" (Fig. 43).

Flying High is Sometimes Better

An Air Force general promised a retiring colonel a nice ride home on the *Geiger* while they were attending a farewell party in London. A few days later, while we were preparing to sail for New York from Southampton, England, the colonel, his spouse, and a large number of bags arrived at the pier. Upon reviewing the medical records, it became clear that the colonel was an insulin-dependent diabetic, and his spouse had undergone a below-the-knee amputation of her left leg several years previously following an accident. Noting this, I tried to explain to the couple, despite what the general had promised, that they both would have to take a plane home. A likely rough winter crossing was medically too risky for each of their medical conditions. (He could become seasick with poor intake, accompanied by vomiting and dehydration, which certainly would aggravate his diabetes. She could fall in rough weather and seriously injure herself.) A series of phone calls arrived from the top brass in London, insisting that it was unlikely there would be any medical problems. Eventually I wound up speaking with the Surgeon General of the Air Force. Our ship's commanding officer was a Navy Lieutenant Commander. He was obviously nervous about all these demands from the top brass in London regarding these two individuals. Standing next to me in the midst of this issue, with his hand trembling, and perspiration on his brow, he scribbled on a piece of paper, "Remember, I'm sticking by your decision." The colonel and his spouse flew back to the States.

Food Problems

Between trips, a Navy physician colleague and I swapped stories about life on the troop transports. He mentioned that he had sent an overweight enlisted man to St. Alban's Naval Hospital prior to his re-enlistment, to determine whether his obesity would prevent his continuing in the service. Three months later, having undergone a host of medical tests, the sailor was discharged from the hospital and reported back for duty. My colleague was a bit puzzled as he related to me that the sailor hadn't lost any weight; in fact he gained 15 pounds!

Toward the end of my sea-time while still on the *Geiger*, a 60-year-old crew member on the way back to the States suffered from a stroke after the ship had been under way for a few days. His prognosis was guarded, and I requested that the Captain steer for the nearest port. Our young Division Officer was overheard discussing where the body could be stored should the patient expire at sea. He sincerely believed that the ice-cream locker would be the best place. It would better preserve the body, and there would be little chance of contamination to the ice cream as the containers were sealed. This suggestion was discounted as the ship's cook might have a cardiac arrest should he open the locker and see a dead man amidst the stored ice cream! Fortunately, the patient was successfully transferred ashore, and our problem was solved.

The Unpredictable Ocean!

One day during a routine trip on the *Geiger*, the ocean was exceptionally rough and caused the ship to do some pretty heavy pitching. The bow would rise on the crest of a large wave and then crash down into the trough of the following wave. The result was predictable: When the bow slammed down, the ship would shudder, and a very large ocean spray would reach the bridge. One of the soldier-passengers decided it would be nice to take a dramatic photo of this scene. As he rounded the corner out of sight of the bridge, a very large wave crashed over the bow as I took a snapshot of the scene. A dim figure can be seen slipping and sliding behind a virtual waterfall. It was the same soldier soaked through to the

Pl. 25

skin. Above the noise made by his sloshing feet in his water-soaked shoes, one could hear him exclaim, "Wow! I didn't think it was so rough!"

A thirty-three-year-old female dependent from Kansas, never having been on a ship before, continued to be in a stage of near hysteria due to the ship's behavior while in the midst of a series of squalls. We admitted her to the ship's hospital for half a day and only a few hours later she would be helped back by a well-meaning fellow passenger. She would pick the center of the cafeteria or the middle of a group of people on deck as a spot for the drama to commence: It was a trophy-winning performance with a well re-hearsed sequence. She would slowly collapse, moan, and breathe heavily; her eyes would close and she would be quickly carried to the dispensary. There were three of these scenarios over two days with no sign of a let-up. It reminded us of a scene from a Holly-wood comedy, since she always managed to have her night clothes in hand while being transported to the dispensary. We gave up dealing with this, and let her stay in the hospital. Only after print-ing a large sign, "Lola's Memorial Bed," firmly fixed and at the foot of her bed did the morale of the medical staff improve.

Every Sunday at sea all of the ship's officers were expected to wear their dress blues or khaki uniforms for Sunday dinner, de-pending on whether it was winter or summer. The chairs and ta-bles in the dining area were fastened to the deck to prevent their being tossed about in rough weather. More than once during the Atlantic crossings, the ship would suddenly go into a sharp roll. Those who were standing and about ready to sit down for dinner could be caught off guard and be sent sprawling across the top of the anchored dinner table, ending up on the deck covered with the cook's choice for Sunday dinner: potatoes, gravy, or whatever the chef had offered us—a humbling experience.

Exposure to the Elements
Tradition has it that the medical officer holds the key to the brandy locker. This goes back to the days of the sailing ships when two or three crewmen might have been unduly exposed to the

"elements" at sea. The idea was that a shot of brandy would "take the chill away." In lieu of a doctor, the captain undoubtedly was in charge of the brandy locker, but in more modern times, on ships that I served, I was entrusted with the key to the locker. Inside there were usually 12 or more 2-oz. bottles of brandy. A log was also kept there, noting each time brandy was dispensed: the date, name of the person(s) given the brandy, and the circumstance. (Sadly, I have learned that this tradition has recently been eliminated.) Nevertheless, one night nearing the end of my year on the *Geiger*, a German freighter sent out a radio message for help from any ship in the area that might have a doctor on board. We altered course to approach the vessel. It was dark and the waves were moderately high. The captain decided to lower a life boat. I joined the crew members as it was also an adventure for me to be in the midst of the Atlantic in the middle of the night. Lowering a lifeboat into the ocean can be tricky as the boat has two falls (a system of pulleys, one in the bow of the boat and the other in the stern) that must be released simultaneously from the ship. If not done correctly, either the bow or the stern of the lifeboat would be tilted up or down. A wave that is rising will create enough slack to unhook both falls together, thus releasing the lifeboat. If the wave is dropping down, the lines holding the lifeboat are stretched tight; and with no slack, the release from the falls is virtually impossible. A deck officer, three or four of the crew, and I entered the boat grasping the ropes that hung down to keep one's balance during the release procedure. Once the lifeboat was successfully released, we motored to the freighter, and, having arrived alongside the freighter, the patient was lowered down to our boat. We then returned with the ill seaman back to our ship. Hooking up the boat to the falls was uneventful, and all went well. The lifeboat was hauled back on board the *Geiger*. The patient had pneumonia, which we treated, and he did well. He was subsequently transferred to a medical facility after we docked in New York. We had good reason for opening the brandy cabinet that night for the lifeboat crew, including myself, as we felt we had been "arguably exposed" to the elements.

Discharge from Active Duty

It was now June 1957. My sea days had come to a close, and it was time to say goodbye to the *Geiger*. My release from active duty was accompanied by my official honorable discharge from the Navy on July 13, 1957. It was time to turn my attention to St. Luke's Medical Center to complete the required three more years of residency training in internal medicine and cardiology and be able to finally begin private practice when I opened my office in Princeton, New Jersey, in July 1960, where I remained in private practice for the next 38 years.

Some Personal Reflections

Whether serving as a deck officer on the bridge or as a medical officer in the ship's dispensary, a set of common denominators is always present: the wonder and uniqueness of each person on board, a definite purpose or goal to be attained, and, not-to-be omitted, the unpredictable and whimsical ocean. Memories of the sea have Pl. 26 always been present since men have sailed the oceans.

Who hasn't been enraptured when gazing upon a star-filled sky on a beautiful summer night while standing alone on the flying bridge? I was fortunate to have enjoyed this spectacle more

Fig. 44. The drama of the sea.

than a few times. The slow, easy roll of the ship seems in tune with the spheres of a peaceful night. During these mystical moments, it is easy to be caught up in the silence and wonder of God's Creation.

On the other hand, the storms and huge waves were also just Pl. 27 as awesome (Fig. 44). Under these conditions, ships will usually steer directly into the waves, for it is better to meet the storm head-on and allow the bow go up and smash down. As mentioned, this pitching of the ship is usually accompanied by the shuddering of the entire vessel, accompanied by a dramatic spray that can cover the bridge. But allowing the waves to strike the vessel broadside may very well result in an excessive roll. More than once, in severe storms, I wondered whether the ship might roll over, a nerve racking experience. The metaphor of storms at sea is much like our personal storms in life. By not rolling over but instead meeting them head-on, and with God's help, we can be sure a peaceful state will be forthcoming in the end. When I was a teenager I chose the sea as my service time. Never would I have dreamed that I would one day consider myself an "old salt."

After 64 Atlantic Ocean crossings, another four in the Pacific, and two voyages in the Caribbean, the old song, "I joined the Navy to see the world, and what did I see? I saw the sea," rings true.

My journeys at sea gave me the unusual opportunity to be in contact with hundreds of people from a host of different backgrounds. And do you know what? People the world over are basically good, and like us, they all have the same hopes for freedom and peace. I am indebted to all of those who were part of any one of the several ships and adventures I was fortunate to experience. We learned a great deal about each other's past cultures and hopes for the future, a living education not found in any textbook.

By now you must realize that there are countless sea stories to be told and many lessons to be learned. Would I like to take one Pl. 28 more trip upon the ocean and to experience the vast, mystical and unpredictable sea? Count me in!

GLOSSARY
(Acronyms and technical terms mentioned in this book)

AP: Auxiliary Passenger vessel. Ship operated by the Navy for non-combat service carrying personnel and cargo.

Beam: Maximum width of a vessel.

"Blow the Tubes": A process of injecting high-pressure steam into the exhaust stack(s) to clear out accumulated soot.

Boatswain: Also bos'n, bo's'n, and bo'sun, bosun. All of these are pronounced bosun. The bos'n has the highest unlicensed rating among the deck crew and immediate charge of all deck hands, overseeing the deck crew, and in charge of the maintenance and upkeep of the ship.

Boom: A horizontal pole or spar attached to the mast or kingpost to which the cargo is fastened during loading and unloading.

Bos'n: *See* Boatswain.

Bulkhead: A wall defining a compartment.

Bunk(s): Bed(s).

BuPers: United States Navy's Bureau of Naval Personnel.

C-1, C-2, C-3, C-4: Types of vessels (progressively increasing in size and carrying capacity).

C.O.: Commanding Officer.

Compartment: Room or space on a ship.

C.V.: Curriculum Vitae (a list of achievements).

Davey Jones Locker: Colorful image referring to the bottom of the sea.

Draft (in a nautical sense): Depth of the vessel below the waterline.

ENT: Ear, Nose, Throat specialist.

Fall (in a nautical sense): The part of the tackle that is hauled upon; a hoisting rope or chain, especially the part of rope or chain to which power is applied.

Fantail: The area of the main deck of a ship that is nearest the stern.

Flying bridge: The highest navigation bridge, which usually includes an added set of controls above the level of the normal control station for better visibility.

Free board on Liberty & Victory ships: The distance from the highest point of the main deck to the waterline. Most often this will vary along the length of the ship. The more buoyant a ship is, the more freeboard will be visible above the waterline for a given weight.

111

"Gadget": My nickname on board the *Catoche*.

Gangplank: A board that forms a bridge from the gangway of a vessel to the wharf or dock.

Gangway: A narrow platform used by persons entering or leaving a vessel moored alongside a pier.

General Quarters: An announcement made aboard a ship to signal the crew to prepare for battle.

Gun tub: An armored structure around a permanently mounted gun aboard ship to protect the gun and gunner from harm.

Hawse Pipe: A structurally reinforced hole in the vessel through which the hawser passes.

Hawser: A steel cable, chain, or large rope for towing or mooring a ship.

Head: Bathroom.

Holiday: Upon completing a paint/cleaning job, a small area that was overlooked.

ICEM: Intergovernmental Committee for European Migration.

Jack: Small flag flown at the bow of the ship when anchored or tied up alongside a pier. See also Union Jack.

Jackstaff: A short mast on the bow of the ship.

Jacob's Ladder: A long rope ladder used to board a vessel at sea.

King Neptune: Legendary God of the Sea. Master of Ceremonies at the celebration of crossing the equator.

Kingpost: A very strong vertical post usually employed as a support for the horizontal load-bearing booms.

Knot: A measure of speed; one knot per hour is a few percent faster than one mile per hour, or 6,076 feet per hour.

K.P.: Kitchen Police. An assignment to wash dishes and/or perform kitchen related duties.

Leeward: Direction away from the wind. Opposite of windward.

Liberty ship: A rapidly constructed vessel built in large numbers during World War II. Precursor to the Victory ship. *See* Victory ship.

M.A.: The Master at Arms, generally a chief or sergeant in charge of keeping rules and order regarding crew or enlisted men.

Magazine: A loaded or unloaded dispenser for ammunition or a storage location for explosives.

MATS: Military Air Transport Service.

MC: Medical Corps.

MSTS: Military Sea Transport Service.

P&S: College of Physicians & Surgeons, Columbia University.

Plebe: First year (freshman) Cadet-Midshipman. During World War II, a Cadet-Midshipman was a "plebe" for only three months.

Pilot: A guide with specific knowledge of a canal, river or other waterway, qualified to steer vessels into or out of harbor.

Pollywog: A mariner who has NEVER crossed the equator. *See* Shellback.

Port: Left side of the ship when facing forward.

R&R: Rest and Recreation (or relaxation).

Rat guard: Circular disc tied to a hawser while ship is docked.

Shellback: A mariner who HAS crossed the equator. *See* Pollywog.

S.P.: Shore Patrol.

SS: Steamship.

Starboard: Right side of the ship facing forward.

Stevedores: Specialists in loading and unloading marine vessels.

TAD: Temporary Assigned Duty.

Tetany: Muscle spasms of the upper extremities and hands due to excess vomiting, dehydration, and hyperventilation.

TV: Tall Vessel.

Union Jack: The American "Union Jack" is a flag flown from the jackstaff. The flag depicts white stars (one star per state) on a blue background.

USAT: United States Attack Transport.

USMM: United States Merchant Marine.

USMMA: United States Merchant Marine Academy.

USNS: United States Navy Ship.

USS: United States Ship. All Navy crew.

Victory ship: Successor to the Liberty ship.

Windward: Towards the wind. Opposite of leeward.

Yardarm: A spar attached to a vertical mast on which signal halyards may be hung.

Zigzag pattern: Patterns of course deviations on timed intervals.

Index

115